The Happy Face Murderer

CW01496997

The Life of Serial Killer Keith Hunter Jesperson

Jack Smith

Disclaimer and Terms of Use

Effort has been made to ensure that the information in this book is accurate and complete. However, the author and the publisher do not warrant the accuracy of the information, text, and graphics contained within the book due to the rapidly changing nature of science, research, known and unknown facts, and internet. The author and the publisher do not hold any responsibility for errors, omissions, or contrary interpretation of the subject matter herein. This book is presented solely for motivational and informational purposes only

Warning

Throughout the book there are some descriptions of murders and crime scenes that some people might find disturbing.

ISBN-13: 978-1530140978

ISBN-10:1530140978

Printed in the United States

MAPLEWOOD
— PUBLISHING —

Contents

Introduction

Stories about serial killers are incredibly popular. Tracking down a mass murderer is a constant plot line in films, television, and literature. But these stories are often based on real life. In certain circumstances, however, real life goes a step beyond what we could imagine happening in fiction. Sometimes, the actions of a serial killer can seem so extreme and strange and their motivations so twisted and evil that we struggle to comprehend exactly how they fit into the modern world. In the case of Keith Hunter Jesperson, the truth behind his murder spree is more horrific than anything Hollywood's best screenwriters could have dreamed up.

After a disturbing childhood left the giant of a man riddled with emotional and psychological scars, Jesperson travelled across Canada and spent time strangling and killing women whom he met along the way. While he was only convicted of eights murders, his own boasts suggest that total could have reached as high as 160. As a truck driver, he had the perfect cover story for travelling from town to town without having to put down roots. Often leaving an unsuspecting family at home, he was out in the wilderness committing heinous acts without anyone from the authorities coming close to suspecting his guilt.

Jesperson, annoyed by the lack of attention he was receiving, began to leave messages to the public. Scrawled onto the walls of truck stop bathrooms, he signed each confession with a happy "smiley face." This led 0the media to christen him the Happy Face Killer. It was decades before the investigators came close to catching the killer. Read on to discover just how Keith Hunter Jesperson managed to get away with way too many horrific murders. This is the story of the Happy Face Killer.

Early Life in Canada

Tracing the life of a serial killer can be a daunting task. Many of the more famous killers, such as John Wayne Gacy or Jeffrey Dahmer, exhibit similar traits and can help point towards a future of deviant behavior. Psychological trauma, abuse, and an inclination towards violence can all hint at what might lie ahead for the young person. In the case of Keith Jesperson, a journey into his childhood can be illuminating, chilling, and prophetic. As we begin to look into exactly what shaped him into the man he became, it becomes increasingly obvious just how distressing a childhood he experienced.

On the 6th of April, 1955, Leslie and Gladys Jesperson gave birth to their third child. The couple lived in a town named Chilliwack in British Columbia, Canada. The boy was named Keith and would eventually be the middle child of five, with two brothers and two sisters. Leslie Jesperson was a stoic man, an alcoholic whose emotional distance from his family would be noted in later years. The distant and often remote Northwest district of Canada has a habit of breeding strong men, but the cold of the climate was bred into Leslie's bones. Out in the wilderness, it was not uncommon to have to endure zero temperature chilling gales, with blizzards regularly forcing the locals indoors. The son of a blacksmith, Leslie Jesperson's father had moved to the region in the 1930s. A failed move to the warmer, more agricultural pastures of Saskatchewan resulted in a humiliating failure for the family, who were some of the millions affected by the aftershocks of the Great Depression. Forced back to the cold, Leslie's family was used to going hungry and to the cold.

The family patriarch, Leslie's father, Arthur, was unfamiliar with the concept of defeat. The failed move to the east and the resigned move back to British Columbia was said to have broken him, embittering him, and forcing him to come to terms with the idea of failure. In the family – descended, they said, from warrior Danes – such losses were abhorrent and not to be tolerated. Arthur's own brother – Keith's great uncle – was committed to an insane asylum around this time. Not wanting to face the idea, he decided to kill himself. Lacking the traditional means, the man took a nail measuring three and a half inches and hammered it into his own skull. This was the family atmosphere in which Leslie was raised and which he would imprint on the young Keith.

The family's blacksmith shop was always busy. There were two forges, and the kids would help out when they weren't in school. Leslie would grow up swinging the hammer against the red hot iron as his father made horse shoes and other metal works for the locals. He worked to the point of exhaustion every day just to help the family put food on the table. By the time Keith was born, the old blacksmith Arthur was relegated to a looming presence in the corner of the room. Rather than the strong-armed iron worker remembered by Leslie and the family, Keith recalled a "tough guy" who never showed emotion to anyone, much less spent time talking to the kids in the family. Women were, to Arthur, seeming wastes of space. The ideas and concepts were impressed upon Leslie and Keith from a young age.

Forever shocked by the failure in Saskatchewan, old Arthur was tainted by the idea that he was forced to sometimes go out and shoot gophers just to feed his family. It was a work ethic and approach to life that left a huge imprint on Keith's father. Leaving school in the tenth grade, Leslie found himself doing anything he could to put together money. Not only was he a plumber and blacksmith, but he took to teaching himself Morse code, mechanical and hydraulic engineering, electronics, and how to manufacture items. During a particularly difficult time, he became a coffin maker for the local native tribes who were suffering from an epidemic. His hard work and creativity left Leslie with a string of clever inventions designed to simplify logging in the area and make it more efficient. Turning his skills to anything, he was able to teach himself how to play the accordion and the keyboard, as well as write poems. Friends of Leslie remembered him as the six-foot-tall life of any party, but the man never topped five foot eleven. The soft rural accent belied a furious anger known only to those closest to him.

Having seen his own father's struggle to piece together a living, Leslie was determined not to let himself be caught in such a rut. As well as being named the Master of the Fraser River Dikes, he took on a number of jobs and started a number of businesses. This time spent on his career impacted the family and the time he was able to spend with his wife and five children. Added to this and above all else, he drank.

To Keith, however, the man was still an icon, a figure demanding respect. Leslie was an engineer, a trusted member of the community, a friend to all who knew him, and he was the family's authority figure. As Keith remembered it at a later date, however, his father would "work and eat and then drink himself to sleep." Just like in the blacksmith's forge, Leslie encouraged – practically demanded – that the children help their father when they could. Every day was a work day, and if the children showed any signs of laziness, they were beaten.

Leslie was a master of both physical and psychological abuse. Keith would remember the sarcastic put-downs, the insults, and the wisecracks made by his father. One incident involved a young Keith asking his father whether an electric fence was working. Leslie encouraged his son to urinate on the fence and laughed uproariously when the boy received a sharp electric shock. He pulled a similar trick with one of the girls, encouraging her to touch the fence while he laughed. As a learned and practical man, Leslie would get angry when his children couldn't replicate his own capacity for learning. He was emotionally and physically distant from the children. Drinking, working, and missing school plays, for example, were all par for the course. Women, too, were also seemingly not deserving of Leslie's respect, with him telling Keith on numerous occasions that he was only still with his wife, Gladys (Keith's mother,) because of her cooking. It was an attitude that Keith would absorb.

Gladys herself was an equally hard worker, but was at least present for the raising of the children. Having been brought up in a strict, puritanical household, she found even the slightest mention of sex abhorrent. When she had been growing up on a farm, the women and girls of the household were not even allowed to be present when the animals were being encouraged to breed. There was not a single member of the Jesperson family – including Leslie – who was ever permitted to see Gladys without her clothes. In her own house, Gladys would allow no discussion of sex, sexuality, or any associated matter. To her, it was an entirely taboo subject. It was a known fact that she preferred the two girls, Jill and Sharon, while Leslie favored two of his boys, Brad and Bruce. Keith was left alone, the forgotten middle child.

For Keith, childhood was not a happy time. Between his father's alcoholic beatings, his mother's staunch religious approach to child rearing, the indifference by both of them, he was encouraged to find his own way in the world. Recognized as the least bright of all of the Jesperson children, Keith's earliest memory is of a day at the park. Standing at the top of the slide and noticing his younger brother Brad sitting at the bottom, he took a decent-sized rock and balanced it at the top of the chute before letting go. The rock rolled down the plastic and caught the younger boy in the head. Blood was drawn, and Brad erupted into a barrage of tears. It would be Keith's sister Sharon who took the blame, however, and he was happy to let her.

People have come forward with memories of Keith's early childhood as being fairly normal. He was a quiet and obedient young boy, but one who was prone to day-dreaming. Facing a lot of teasing about his inability to focus and his lack of mental athleticism, Keith was a ponderous, sluggish young boy. The only area where he showed any capacity was in the family's favorite game, cribbage, which he was able to play before he could read.

During the time of Keith's childhood, Chilliwack was a rural area. Though the family would later move to the larger town of

Selah, they would always own animals, including chickens, horses, ducks, sheep, and dogs. Leslie, ever the handyman, built a wooden water wheel to help trap salmon in the stream that would run through their land. As the children were out helping and working, they would be scattered across the several acres the family owned. When it was time for dinner, Gladys would pull the cord on a huge orange whistle, and the children would come running back to the kitchen table.

Keith was also a shy boy. Happy to play alone, even before he started school, he could be found digging tunnels and building forts. His mother thought that he was never happier than when playing alone. Daydreaming and imagining his life as a hunter in Africa or a sailor in the navy, Keith played out heroic fantasies in his mind, but always on his own.

But sometimes, it was impossible to escape his father's attention. Speaking after his imprisonment, Keith could recall one day when he was forced into hiding under the kitchen table from the leather belt that Leslie used to whip the children. As his father screamed, "Don't you run away from me!" the then four year old attempted to hide amid the chair and table legs. Grabbed and dragged out, Leslie laid the belt repeatedly across his son's backside, punishment for some long-forgotten indiscretion. Stop crying, Keith was told, or he would be given something to cry about.

One incident that Keith remembered incurring his father's wrath involved a duck that Leslie kept as a pet. Keith had been playing outside when he came across the bird, a favorite of his father's various menagerie. Suddenly struck by a violent impulse, Keith took a rock and killed the bird. His father found out, and despite Gladys's attempts to intervene, Keith received a whipping with the belt. The drink consumed by Leslie gave the beating an extra edge and made him almost impossible to reason with when his temper flared.

Keith would find a friend before he was five years old. A brown Labrador named Duke arrived in the house just before Keith's birthday and soon became firmly attached to the middle child. Sharing a room with Brad, Duke could often be found sleeping on Keith's bed during the nights. For once, Keith had a topic he was happy to discuss with anyone. He would animatedly chat about Duke with anyone who would listen. The dog would chase salmon along the stream and cars along the road, taking a few blows in the process. Duke would chase off rival dogs and even killed two of the neighbor's dogs who might have ventured into the yard. Protective of Keith, Duke would shield him from any intruders onto the property. This was where Keith got his first insight into the reproductive ways of the world, with Duke attempting to have sex with any female dog he came across. Keith later joked that the dog gave him a "head start about sex."

When Keith did try to make friends, however, things did not proceed in the best of fashions. He was often teased for being taller and more cumbersome than the other children at school. One attempt to befriend a Native American child resulted in Leslie becoming angry and telling Keith to break off any relationship with the boy, as there was simply nothing to be gained from the friendship. A school sports day ended in disaster when a hop, skip, and jump event involved Keith. Rather than running before launching himself forwards, Keith simply stood in one spot, hopped, skipped, and then jumped. The teacher pointed out his efforts as the exact opposite of the desired technique, the other children burst into laughter, and Keith ran home, telling himself that he didn't need anyone else.

His parents attempted to find a friend for Keith, and a boy named Martin would occasionally be welcomed to the home. Martin was a troublesome boy, who would find ways to create mischief and leave Keith saddled with the blame. The clumsy child, too tall for his age, near-sighted and not especially bright, Keith found few ways in which to escape the punishments Martin's behavior brought his way. Subjected to beatings and punishments in front of everybody, one day Martin's actions grew too much for Keith. Keith tracked the boy down and trapped him in the space behind the family's garage. Keith jumped on the youngster, wrapping his hands around Martin's neck. He choked and choked, refusing to let go until Leslie arrived on the scene and pulled him away. By the time Keith relinquished his grip, Martin was unconscious. If his father had not arrived, Keith admits that the boy would likely have become his first victim. Once again, Keith received a beating. This time, he knew he was guilty.

Discussing the event later, Keith Jesperson remembers that this was the first time he was able to envisage himself as two distinct people. The normal, gentle side of his personality stood by and watched as the angrier side took control. This added to the imaginary world into which the boy would often retreat, something he named "Keith's World." In this place, he was able to retreat from the difficulty of everyday life and spend his time with animals, away from antagonists such as his brothers and his classmates.

Keith's relationship with animals was complicated. As well as Duke, whom he loved, and the other family pets, Keith once came across a raven with a broken wing. He picked up the bird, splintered its wing, and made a home for it out of rags. He named the bird Blackie. Arriving home from school one day, Keith discovered that his older brother and a friend had taken the bird and trapped it under an orange milk crate. They hurled their pocket knives at the bird until it died, all while Keith watched. Furious, he ran into his brother's room and threw all of the toy planes out of the window. Leslie was unimpressed, saying Blackie was just a "dumb crow." Keith was punished, Bruce was not.

But animals' deaths were not unfamiliar to Keith. He would help his father out around the land, killing gophers on a regular basis. He would arrive home covered in gopher blood after an enjoyable day's hunting. Leslie could not abide the presence of too many cats on the farm. When kittens were born, they were killed quickly. Keith would help, much to his sisters' disgust. Similarly, he was taught how to deal with garter snakes that were found on the property, taking a hoe and cutting the reptiles in two. But this often wasn't enough. Keith admits that he "enjoyed" watching them struggle as he balanced the blade on their backs, even going as far as to torture the animals with garden tools. For young Keith, it was just one more way of having fun.

Alongside various stories of torturing animals and disagreements with other children, Keith was aware of sex from an early age. As is perhaps inevitable for someone growing up in a rural area, the animals gave some insight for the young boy, providing ideas that were carried over into a relationship with a little girl. When Keith was five, he had his first kiss on the back seat of his mother's car. The two continued their experiments and "practiced sex," which for the children meant kissing, a little bit of inquisitive touching, and showing one another the more private areas of the body. If Gladys had ever discovered her child in such a position, she would likely have been furious.

Sex presented itself in Keith's life in an entirely more dubious fashion when he was playing on a neighbor's farm. While he and some other children entertained themselves, one of the workers offered to teach them about sex. He encouraged the children to undress and did likewise, before encouraging them to touch one another. Keith quickly grew scared and ran away before anything could happen. Later, he would ask one of the boys who had been left behind what had occurred. He was told that the dairy worker had sodomized the youngster, that it had hurt, and that the boy had told his father. The boy's parents encouraged their son to keep quiet, but the worker was never seen again on the farm.

Friendships with the local boys were always fractious. Despite being the same age, in the same class, and living right next door to one boy, Keith managed to provoke nothing but ire in the child. Keith was often bullied by the boy, punched and hit almost every time they met one another. This culminated in another close call when, with the pair swimming at nearby Cultus Lake one summer, the boy took Keith by the head and held him under the surface of the lake, briefly allowed him up to breath, then forced him back down again. This went on for ten minutes, until Keith could see nothing but black. He was saved when a counsellor jumped in the water and pulled him out. But vengeance would be had. When the pair visited a local swimming pool, Keith grabbed the boy by the head and thrust it underwater. Keith was always the bigger, stronger one of the pair, though rarely knew how to use his size advantage. This time, however, he took advantage of his size and held the boy underwater with every intention of letting him die. The boy was only saved when a lifeguard dragged Keith away. It was the second murder attempt of a young life.

As Keith grew older, his interests grew more complicated. After briefly making friends with some boys in the area, he began to learn various techniques for torturing animals. They would attach firecrackers to sparrows, nail crows to a wooden board as throwing knife target practice, or would feed Alka-Seltzer to seagulls, a practice which would make the birds' stomachs burst inside them. But the torture was not limited to birds. Keith and his cohorts would take cats and dogs, nailing them to the same boards and fill them with needles and other sharp objects. Keith still recalls one of his favorite pastimes, which involved crimping together cats' tails using wire, throwing them over either side of a rope, and watching until one clawed the other to death. The boys would sit and laugh. Even after one cat had died, the other would still yelp, howl, and scream until it died of its wounds. The boys found it uproariously funny.

Living in America

At the age of twelve, Keith was informed by his parents that they would be moving to Washington State in the US. Leslie had been approached by an American group who wanted him to design machinery on their hop farm. Despite the fact that Keith had experienced a difficult upbringing in Canada, the thought of moving to the States terrified him. He didn't want to leave Canada. He knew the area. He had a paper route. This didn't matter, of course, and the family was soon leaving Chilliwack for Selah, Washington. They moved into a large home in a middle class neighborhood. But just like back in Canada, Keith was unable to get too close to anyone. While he had been a little bit strange and different in Canada, he was considered downright odd in America.

Keith's sister Jill recalls the effect the move had on her brother, suggesting that it changed him. He began to acquire nicknames, always referring to his large frame. Sloth. Fatty. Hulk. Tiny. But they never seemed to bother Keith that much. The real change Jill remembers was in her older brother's humor, which took a turn towards darker subjects. He would laugh at the disgusting, the morbid. He went out exploring with Duke and had soon tracked out about five miles in every direction from the family home. He was always playing by himself.

One incident saw Keith and the closest thing he had to a friend – a boy named Tom Haggar – caught shoplifting. The pair were paraded around in front of their classmates by the police, taken back to the station, and had their fingerprints taken. When Keith eventually told his parents, he was sent to his room, while Leslie phoned Tom's parents. Leslie was informed that Keith had been the mastermind behind the enterprise, a concept that Leslie found unsurprising. Keith was driven to the store the next day and made to apologize. He was told to clean out the back alley behind the store as a punishment. His father would, for a long time afterwards, refer to Keith as his "little thief." Throughout the town, Keith now had a reputation as a corrupting influence. Any friends he had made were now banned from seeing him.

By the time Keith moved into the eighth grade, he was fully ensconced in Keith's World. He lived in his daydreams, without the troublesome friends that he had found so difficult to acquire. Thoughts and ambitions were entertained, especially with the view to becoming a mounted police officer back in Canada, one of the famous Mounties. One slight issue pertaining to this matter was Keith's physical fitness, which was lagging far behind what was required of the Canadian police recruits. An encounter with a distant relative brought the youngster into contact with experiences from the Vietnam War, wherein Keith looked over photos and listened to experiences of soldiers who had killed and tortured the enemies. The ideas brought back memories of Keith's time torturing animals, which he later admitted provided him with sexual pleasure.

In Selah, however, there were fewer targets open to his impulses. Stray dogs and cats were not nearly as abundant as they had been back in Chilliwack. One time, when chasing down a tomcat with his BB gun, Keith managed to corner the animal. It was shot full of pellets until it couldn't move, so the boy moved in with a stone and smashed the cat's paws. He remembers that it took fifty-six BB pellets before the cat finally died.

As he moved into adolescence, however, one of the major problems in Keith's life was left unrequited. The opposite sex presented him with many problems. Often, he would approach girls only to be rejected before he'd even finished his sentence. Always busy at his father's work place, he found himself admiring women from a distance and rarely spending any time in their company. After a few embarrassing fumbles with older girls during a trip to Canada, he decided that he would spend some time researching sex. After looking into various books on the subject, he found himself assuming the role of victim in any potential encounter and mixed the concept of sexual intercourse with rape. When writing about his first sexual encounter, he described the girl who climbed on top of him as having "raped me over and over."

Despite the interactions and experiences he had meeting girls while away in Canada, getting to know any in Selah seemed an entirely different prospect. In the area, he had acquired the nickname "Igor" and "Ig" for short. The name-calling was led by his older brother Brad, who teased and taunted Keith during the move up to high school, where Brad was already a student. Other students picked on the boy, still big for his age. They asked for loans and to borrow items. They rarely had any intention of returning anything. Keith was happy to yield rather than to fight back and get in trouble once again.

Attempts were made to turn his size into something productive. Noticing that the school athletes all impressed the girls, he tried to take part in the football team. Already six foot, two inches and over two hundred pounds, it seemed like a natural fit. Keith resented having to play tackle or guard however, believing these to be "dumb" positions. When the coach encouraged him to "kill" the opposition, he bluntly replied that he would do no such thing. Keith, worried about hurting his teammates in practice, was wary from the outset. When he did get to play in a game against another school, Keith charged into the fray, nearly broke one player's leg, and then smashed two of the quarterback's ribs. Keith was dismissed from the game. The coach was impressed, but Keith was perturbed by the idea of working on a team. The perpetual loner, he quit the team. Wrestling was another brief interest and a more individual sport. But Keith's parents never turned out to watch any of his games. Gladys might arrive for one or two, but never with the enthusiasm shown when any of the other children were participating.

Growing older, Keith Jesperson became more and more exposed to alcohol. With his father already a committed alcoholic, those around him were also beginning to indulge themselves to a greater extent and presented Keith with something of a temptation. Leslie responded to such temptation among his kids by allowing them to drink what they liked as long as they were at home. He sought to remove the glamour and the allure of alcohol and, as Keith remembers, he succeeded. The older brothers would have keg parties at the family home on occasion, events that took on a large level of local notoriety. Keith recalls attending one, getting drunk, and attempting to grope a girl who would later turn out to be his brother's date.

When he turned sixteen, Keith passed his driving test and finally had a means to travel independently further than he could walk. His first car was a brown sedan which he drove until it broke down, and his second car was a Jeep. Gas was always in short supply, and the teenager topped up what he could afford by siphoning fuel out of other people's gas tanks. The freedom of a car allowed Keith to cater to his compulsions. He would be able to drive out into the wilderness with his .22 rifle and shoot at what he found.

By the time Keith was a junior in Selah, his dog Duke was starting to get old. Rather than the boundless companionship of earlier days, Keith now needed to help the dog up into his bed at night, up on to the sofa when they watched TV, and had to care for the dog's arthritic limbs as it moved around the family home. Les Jesperson was never a fan of Duke. The dog, he thought, was stupid, useless for hunting, but Keith loved Duke regardless. One day, he came home from school and was informed by one of the workers on the farm that Duke had died. Distraught, Keith tracked down his father, who played off the death with the suggestion that the dog must have eaten some coyote poison and had grown ill. Les had been forced to shoot him. To Keith, this was essentially murder.

Duke was not the only dog in the Jesperson household, but he was the only one Keith loved. After he died, Keith turned his angry attention to the dogs his father liked better. He would sneer and snarl at them and hit them when they got too close. The other dogs learned not to spend too much time around Keith and would often go running as soon as he entered the room. One of the dogs was so scared that it would urinate whenever Keith came near. Another grew so scared on one occasion that it bolted out into the middle of the road, running away from Keith, whereupon it was hit by a passing car.

Sex still played on Keith's mind. He had matured past his awkward youth and was considered something of a handsome, strapping man. Tall and strong, he was still socially misguided. He found some relief through pleasuring himself, which he found to be easier than the circus around talking to girls. Inevitably, anyone who showed interest in him seemed to want to use him as either a source of money or a means of transport. Outside of the social circle and male comradery he might have expected, he was unable to turn to his peers for advice on interacting with the opposite sex.

Asking his parents or brothers seemed out of the question. Thoughts and daydreams began to revolve around rape and kidnapping, of overpowering a smaller girl in order to discover the as-yet-unknown world of sex.

By the time he reached his senior year in high school, the prospect of having a girlfriend had all but evaporated from Keith's mind. His sex life was a solitary affair. That was until he met a girl in the year below, a junior whom he thought to be cute and, shockingly to Keith, seemed to like him back. After a few dates and days out at the local drag races, Keith settled into a pattern with the girl as something of a steady girlfriend.

Wrestling was still an outlet for Keith. As a fully-fledged member of the team, he was technically part of the athletic elite at the high school. There were still ambitions and dreams in the back of his mind revolving around returning to Canada to join the Mounties. In better shape physically, he might even stand a chance of passing their tests. One day, the coach arranged for a rope trial. The students were to climb to the top of the rope as fast as they could. A big teenager, Keith had never managed the feat. Still teased about his size and his clumsiness, such a trial seemed impossible for "Igor." But on this particular occasion, Keith dragged himself all the way to the top. Once he reached the pinnacle, the fastenings began to falter and snapped. Keith fell from twenty-five feet onto the hard floor. There was a sharp pain shooting through the left side of his body. Unable to move, Keith writhed in agony as he was told to get up and walk it off. Assisted, he rose to one foot and limped to the showers.

The coach eventually agreed to call Gladys, and an increasingly dizzy Keith was rushed to the emergency room in an ambulance. After several X-rays and help from his older sister Sharon, who was a nurse, Keith was told he had a nasty sprain but would be up again in a couple of weeks. This wouldn't be the case. A few days later, Keith's left foot swelled up to double its size. He had to rip open a boot to force his foot inside. His girlfriend stopped calling, so he braved the pain and drove to her house. Once there, the girl's mother said that Keith wasn't welcome and no one wanted to see him. Despite the relationship, the mangled foot of Keith Jesperson was too much for the girl. Limping was now common, and any attempt to wrestle was met with opponents deliberately going for his injured foot. All trips to the country to kill animals were put on hold, all potential dates with girls forsaken. Keith cut a larger slit down the side of his boot for his swollen foot and returned to work in his dad's business. Now, he really did fit the "Igor" nickname.

School turned out to be a bust for Keith, who graduated with unimpressive grades. College was out of the question, seemingly, while occasional thoughts of a military career were entertained and rejected. His foot still bothered him, though he took a job pumping gas. Foot trouble continued until he went to see a specialist, whereupon Keith was eventually diagnosed with torn ligaments. This meant needing arch support initially, then three surgeries. For the three months after the first operation, Keith was resigned to crutches. Work turned to more sedate, inside jobs while he recovered, during which time there were considerations of whether or not it would be feasible to sue the school board. He moved in and out of the family home, especially when Leslie Jesperson borrowed Keith's motorbike and drunkenly crashed, landing himself in critical care. Keith was charged with the family business while his father recovered. As well as the accident wounds, Les was told he needed to quit drinking lest the alcohol kill him. Struggling, Les told people that it was for his family that he kicked the habit, though Keith knew better.

Romance was still an issue, while the surgeries and foot issues had put an end to Keith's ambition of joining the Mounties. Aged nineteen, working in the family business, and still not entirely recovered, his life appeared listless and directionless. But a wrong order at a fast food restaurant led to him meeting a seventeen year old named Rose. The pair flirted, dated, and eventually got engaged. Rose's mother didn't trust Keith, while Keith's family constantly reiterated just how lucky he was to have met this girl. For Rose, marriage to Keith seemed like the best way out of a busy household. They were set to marry on her eighteenth birthday, despite Keith's misgivings. On the 2nd of August, 1975, Keith Jesperson married Rose Pernick. Thus, with mixed feelings and an amateur appreciation of romantic relationships, the Happy Face Killer was married and began a new chapter in his life, one that would eventually lead down an ever more twisted road.

Married Life

For the future serial killer, life as a married man was entirely different to what he had experienced before. A job with a lumber company beckoned, but the constant need for surgery on his foot kept Keith close to his parents, working in his father's various workshops when he could. Rose was beginning to discover that life away from her family was not as blissful as she had imagined. The pair moved into a mobile home, which they parked on a part of the Jesperson estate that had been turned into the "Silver Spur Mobile Park." Together with his father, Keith operated the heavy machinery and carried out the work needed to turn a plot of land into a trailer park ready for over a hundred mobile homes. Numbers began to swell as residents moved in. Les was sure to be strict with residents, while Keith took a friendlier approach. Perhaps too friendly, it might have seemed, as his father could recall an instance where a soon-to-be-evicted tenant with a teenage daughter mentioned the possibility of calling the cops, with the charge of statutory rape on her mind. Keith shrugged off the suggestion, but he does remember watching women through the windows of their trailers at night, before returning to his home to fantasize while in bed with his wife about what he had seen.

But the base instincts were never far away. Even when he was busy working at the trailer park, Keith felt the need to return out to the wilderness and find something to kill. With a set of by-laws on the park to guard against strays, Keith one day encountered a cat on the property where he had had trouble before. He picked up the creature and slammed it into the pavement. Picking up the stunned cat, he wrung its neck, and then drove out a few miles to fling it from the window of his car. The tenant was told that the cat had simply run away.

Animals that Keith deemed to be pests were taken out in a variety of ways. While Les has resigned himself to drowning the occasional stray cat in a sack, his son would use anything he had available. Shovels, screwdrivers, sickles, scythes, hammers, or simply his bare hands. He would shoot dogs with his pistol or simply throw them out of the window of a speeding car. A dog rummaging through his garbage was beheaded with a scythe (the blade only managed to cut through half of the neck,) while poisoned meat was used to kill seven cats and kittens in just one night. Other cats were burned alive in an incinerator, or trapped in a barrel with gasoline before Keith threw a match in afterwards. Later, he would admit to deriving an almost sexual pleasure from the act of killing.

Eventually, Keith's court case against the school regarding his horrific injury was finally settled. In 1976, he was awarded $33,000 in a settlement. For Keith, this seemed like the chance to finally move back to Chilliwack. Instead, Les managed to convince his son to invest the money in expanding the trailer park. They would be business partners, with Keith and Rose owning ten percent. Rose could even be put in charge of the books. Keith agreed and went about the work of laying concrete for the expansion.

Following the business proposal, Rose began to pressure Keith for children. The idea perturbed Keith, who knew himself to still be attracted to other women, one in particular named Arliss who was a member of his bowling team. After being turned round to the idea by Rose, six months of attempting to conceive bore no results. On checking with a doctor, it was found Keith had a low sperm count. He blamed the stress of his living and working arrangements, especially the influence of his father. Rose, desperate for children, even put the couple on an adoption list.

The dream of the Silver Spur Mobile Home Park did not last. After only two years, money problems forced the family to sell. Spending what money he had from the sale on a series of poor ventures, Keith found that he needed money fast. He took a series of low paying jobs, often all at once. Eventually, he managed to secure a position at a local trucking company. The idea of being an independent truck driver appealed to Keith, and this was his first step along the path. It began with working in the garage, welding, repairing, and performing other tasks. Away from the stress of the trailer park and working sixty hours at his new job, Keith became a father for the first time. Melissa was born in 1979, into a household still experiencing money troubles, but she was well-loved by her parents.

A year later, Jason was born. Keith doted on the children. When they were around their grandfather, Les, Keith was adamant that he should never touch them. Keith never beat his children, and was sure that his father wouldn't either. Keith's beatings and humiliations at his father's hands still festered under the surface of their cordial relationship.

Soon, Keith was driving trucks. His assignments were getting to be longer and longer, with Keith spending more and more time behind the wheel, away from his young family. At this point, he was only present some five or six days every four weeks. This took a toll on the marriage. Arguments began to abound, and tempers frayed. Rose had put on weight during her pregnancy, a fact that Keith was sure to mention. Their libidos were running at different speeds, with Keith's urge to rush to the bedroom on their first meeting not in line with Rose's desires of how to spend what little family time they had.

Even when out driving the truck, Keith was still something of a prisoner to his urges. Sometimes he might start a random fire, or attack a stray cat, even in front of his children. Similarly, old feelings of distance began to creep back into his life as he found it tough to make friends with those in the same business. In Canada, he was viewed as American. In America, he seemed Canadian. So, in 1981, after Keith discovered a new spate of jobs opening up in British Columbia, he moved the family back north of the border. Rose, pregnant once again, was less than enthusiastic. She would follow once Keith was settled in the new home.

Finally, Keith was free. Free from his parents and his father's influence over his life. Free from the rigorous work schedules that locked him down to one place. Even free from his wife and children. Out on the road, he was independent. This was put to the test soon, when an effervescent Keith decided to pull over and help a young girl on the side of the road. She was having trouble with her car. A quick check under the bonnet revealed that it was a simple fix. Delighted, the attractive young girl gave Keith her number and promised to buy him dinner in Spokane. Keith refused the temptation to stray from his martial vows, but he pulled to the side of the road a short while later and masturbated to the image.

It didn't take long for Keith to settle in Canada. He started out by waving flags on site, but was soon driving the coal trucks. In the bottom of the coal pits, the huge trucks that moved the produce weighed up to 170 tons when fully loaded. Driving them around the quarry was dangerous work. If the brakes failed on an incline, the driver was told to drag his truck along the side of the wall in an attempt to slow the vehicles down.

This work was great for Keith's long-term goal of cross country trucking adventures. And away from the family, getting to know his new work colleagues, Keith found himself even enjoying his bachelor lifestyle.

But this came to a shuddering halt when Rose and the kids arrived. The family took a two bedroom flat, and Rose made her annoyance at Keith's new misadventures known. Scared he might lose his kids, Keith reeled in his behavior. Jason, Melissa, and the newborn Carrie were very, very important to Keith. But trouble was always just around the corner and, as usual, the relationship between Keith and his father was to blame.

In British Colombia, the real money was in welding. Abandoning his trucking dreams to focus on the large debts he had racked up, Keith retrained as a welder and was soon making good money. But he noticed that everyone around him in the workshop was stealing. Batteries, tools, even engine parts. Everything seemed to go missing, and everyone seemed to be in on the heist. Eventually, Keith was too.

Meanwhile, Les had opened a hardware store back in America. Speaking over the phone, he casually mentioned how nice the leather overalls were that they had in Keith's workshop. Soon, the son was on the lookout for a set in his father's size. A guard posted at the door caught him as he tried to smuggle the clothes out of the shop. Keith was offered a deal: admit the theft and have it all forgotten about in a year.

Les advised Keith to deny everything, lest everyone at the company assume he was a thief. Keith, against his better judgement, took his father's advice. He denied everything and was fired. After the good money he had been making in the welding shop, he chose to blame his father once again for his current, precarious predicament.

The next two years were spent looking for a job in Canada. None paid as well as the welding position. Truck driving was back on the cards, but it paid a fraction of the wages. The family moved a hundred miles east to escape any possible rumors about Keith's dismissal. A brief stint as the driver of a huge Peterbilt machine allowed him to control a dream machine, but company layoffs hit after only eight months. A fleeting interest in boxing helped Keith get back into shape, but the cold Alberta weather caused Rose to complain. Soon, news arrived that Gladys had contracted lymph-node cancer. To bring the grandchildren back near their dying grandmother, the whole family moved back to the south. Rose was happy, but Keith was not. It seemed that, though he loved his kids, Keith had fallen out of love with his wife.

With money still tight, the family bought a home. Keith had a trucking job, but nothing to fall back on if he lost it. Les offered to help with the down payment on the mobile home, a move which Keith saw as just another attempt to exert control. But these days, Keith was too busy to argue. He was too busy, still, to indulge his violent fantasies. There were no chances to drive out to the middle of nowhere to dismember a cat or to torture a dog. There was no time to set fires. He had to work.

This meant driving trucks all across the state, and it was something that Keith, finally, liked. At times, he was essentially living in the truck, away from the family. Out on the road, there was no one to criticize or complain to him. In Keith's view, he was the master of his fate, the king of his domain. As an extra benefit, there was always a slew of available women present in the regular truck stop haunts. While he was still adamant about staying "true" to Rose, Keith saw no crime in looking at other women when he was out of town. In every stop, Keith would flirt with the waitresses in the diners and cafes. No longer finding his relationship with Rose sexually gratifying, leaving Keith with masses of stored-up tension in need of release. This meant, at first, bike rides or hikes, attempts to make himself too tired to pursue sex with his wife.

One day, Keith arrived back from a trucking journey to learn that his mother's cancer had grown worse. She died two weeks later, after Keith came to visit her on her deathbed. At the funeral, several people noted that Keith was not showing any real, explicit emotion. When looking back over their fuss, he failed to see the problem. His mother was "just ashes." Within a year, Les would be remarried.

In 1986, Keith faced his worst fear. He lost his trucking job after the boss's son took his place. This made mortgage repayments a problem, and the family soon had to move. Again, Keith was back to juggling part-time jobs, trying to get by on caffeine, sugary drinks, and not enough sleep. At times, he even stole from the bar where he was working as a doorman. Eventually, it got to be too much. Rose accidently overdrew the family bank account, and Keith was furious. Determined not to beat his wife (or his children) as his father might have done, he unleashed his rage on the front door. A big hole was punched through the wood. Rose left for a few hours to allow her husband to cool down. The door was never fixed, existing as a perpetual reminder, Keith thought, to think before writing a check. But it was no good. Eventually, the family declared bankruptcy.

Eventually, Keith found another trucking job. Once again, he was free to travel up and down the state. But his sexual frustration found no release. That was until he chanced upon an encounter with the wife of a friend. After dropping little Jason off to play with the friend's son, the father – Billy – made his excuses and left. As soon as he was gone, the mother – Ginny – began to make advances for Keith. He played them off, worried about Billy finding out. When Billy arrived back home, Keith's confession was met with indifference. The couple were swingers. Confused but interested, Keith had sex with Ginny that night and many time afterwards. It was the first time he cheated on Rose, and he only stopped after Billy and Ginny moved away from the area.

From then on, the seal on Keith's promiscuity seemed to have broken. After fantasizing about the women he met while driving his truck, and never skipping an opportunity to assist a damsel in distress on the side of the road, Keith began to pick up a series of mistresses. The divorcee he met in a late-night restaurant. The two young girls who wanted to see inside his truck. Anyone but the prostitutes who frequented the truck stops. They were considered a step too far. Keith liked to assume that his moral compass was still very firmly pointed towards the good, in actions if not in thoughts.

But this wouldn't last long. One night saw Keith and his truck travelling down Highway 97. His lights picked out the shape of a young girl pushing along a bicycle in the middle a storm. Pulling over, he offered her a lift. She was young – possibly around fifteen – and of Native American descent. She reminded Keith of the young girls who had lived near his home in Chilliwack. Already, his fantasies were running wild with ideas. Driving along, he imagined taking her by force. Picking a parking spot, he reached over before he could even completely park the truck. The girl seemed to have predicted such an attack and leaped out of the cabin.

The girl was fifty feet away, and Keith had no hope of catching her. Trying to play off the incident, he returned the girl's bike and sped away as fast as he could. For the next month, he was terrified of being caught. All the possible means of identification flashed through his head – the license plate, the load, his somewhat unique appearance – and he imagined the girl informing her father of the attempted rape. But nothing happened. Keith swore to stick only to girls who wanted to have sex with him. Or his wife.

After a few months of renewed sexual frustration, Keith was back to familiar targets. A cat received a stoning in front of Jason, and Keith drowned a neighbor's dog when he was all alone. He took particular care in the latter, allowing the dog up to breath occasionally to prolong the act. It was a technique he found satisfying in a sexual fashion and one he would use later on. Animals were always under threat from Keith, and his children knew it. He might douse a cat in water and throw it out into the freezing night, or cover a dog in gasoline and throw it a lit match. Even his children's own dog was not safe. After it developed hemorrhoids, Keith took it out into the back yard and smashed the little dog's head. The children cried for days.

Following the incident with the girl who got away – and noting his growing frustrations – Keith decided that he might need to try professional assistance. Out in his truck once again, Keith met Linda, a prostitute. He spent twenty dollars for three hours of Linda's attentions. She was the first of a string of girls as Keith got more and more accustomed to paying for sex. There was a woman in almost every truck stop, dotted along the various routes. When he arrived back home to Rose, he might try to gauge her interest in romantic activity, but she was never able to satisfy his burning urges. One time, Rose asked to come along on one of the trips. The trip was no fun, culminating in her husband pushing her towards a pair of pimps in one truck stop and joking that they could take her. Once they arrived home, Keith immediately went to the irrigation ditch behind the house and drowned a cat. With scratches up his arms, he told the watching children that it had "got in his way." After that, people started to grow worried for Keith's state of mind. In all, it was the beginning of the end of their happy marriage.

It was with the marriage in this state that Keith met Peggy Jones. A waitress in a truck stop who flirted with Keith and eventually went back to his cabin, Peggy was the first woman who Keith met who could keep up with his sexual urges. A few weeks after meeting her, he called her again. Then again. And again. Soon, he was stopping at her home every time he went out on the road. He told Peggy that he wasn't married, and she told him she was going through a divorce. Soon, Keith was spending more time with the new woman than he was with his family. After a short time, Peggy and Keith began to see themselves as a couple and took trips together. The told one another that they were each in love with the other. Peggy advised Keith that he needed to finish his marriage and break away from the father he was always complaining about.

Driving Peggy up to a tavern near his home, Keith went back to the family. Before going to bed, he played with the kids for a few hours. When lying next to Rose, he told her that he wasn't happy, that he wanted a divorce. His wife rolled to one side and went to sleep. No arguments, no disagreements. In the morning, Keith played with the kids again and Rose remained silent. He left to drive his rig south and, when he returned, he found an empty home and a letter informing him that Rose and the kids had gone to live with her mother in Spokane. She wanted everything in the divorce, everything except Keith's bowling ball, his golf clubs, his bicycle, and his clothes. Keith read the letter and sat down and cried.

In the summer of 1988, Keith decided that he might need to turn to his sister Jill for advice. Driving to her place in Seattle, he was involved in a traffic accident and found himself in the hospital. Unable to work, he lost his job. Taking a new position with shorter journeys, Keith discovered that he could smuggle Peggy along for the ride. Despite her waitressing job, she was happy to attend. The manager at her workplace warned Keith against the girl, telling him that she flirted with all of the truckers who came in and very nearly rode off with some of them. Keith ignored the man. He moved in with Peggy and enjoyed, for the first time, living with a woman who enjoyed sex as much as he did.

But nothing else was quite so rosy. The kids were far away, and keeping up with the child support was proving difficult. Money was in increasingly short supply, and Les wasn't helping, having taken a dislike to Peggy. Keith, always one to take the contrarian view to whatever his father suggested, refused to listen to his father's advice to return to his family. The divorce was finalized on the couple's thirteenth anniversary. Keith would later confess that getting involved with Peggy would prove to be an awful mistake. Losing his family in such a fashion was an even worse mistake.

Life with Peggy quickly lost its sheen. After being together a year, the couple decided that they might benefit from being on the road together. Keith put in the papers to make Peggy his official driving partner. In his fantasy, they could get twice as much work done, and he would be able to have sex as often as he liked. But Keith underwent a sudden change of mind. Whether it was his dad's constant suggestions or guilt about his family, Keith told Peggy to leave and began to make plans to go back to his family. The pair had a goodbye drink just before Keith left. After popping out of the mobile home for a few hours, Keith returned to discover the TV smashed and Peggy passed out on the bed in front of him. He was overcome with his urges.

Removing her shoes and clothes, Keith proceeded to have sex with the sleeping woman. He did so multiple times before leaving to sleep at his dad's house. When he met up with Peggy in the morning, she asked whether they had had sex. Keith admitted they had, but left out the details of the rape. He left to be with his family for the next two and a half weeks. But he couldn't get Peggy out of his head. Despite realizing how much he'd missed his family, Keith couldn't bear to leave behind the sexual gratification that Peggy offered. He chose to return to her and leave his family once again.

The move to make Peggy a co-driver was made official, but Keith soon found that it was less than ideal. Peggy was not a skilled or committed driver. She couldn't work the truck in difficult conditions, resented being given navigational advice, and refused to work the long hours Keith was used to. This meant that he was forced to do a huge majority of the driving, especially in anything resembling tricky conditions. Meanwhile, Peggy would flirt with other truckers over the CB radio. Soon enough, the boss as the trucking company decided that Peggy was a hindrance more than a help and removed her from the rotation.

Keith snuck his girlfriend back into the truck anyway. But he could never rely on her to help with driving. Peggy had no sense of direction and no road smarts. He would take a nap in the bed and, when he woke up, would find that they were parked in a truck stop, miles off course. Peggy would be inside, flirting with the other truckers. When one offered to take her off Keith's hands, he readily agreed. This resulted in Peggy chasing him out into the parking lot, begging forgiveness. They continued this way for a year. Despite all the difficulties presented by the arrangement, Keith was at least happy to be having sex three times a day.

The couple ran into trouble when Keith was laid off from his job. Suffering an injury around the same time, he was unable to work. Now armed with a license, Peggy took to the roads as a trucker. Keith began to hear from his friends that she was perpetually unfaithful and that he would be wise to dump her as quickly as possible.

By the time 1990 rolled around, the pair were nearly finished. When Peggy informed Keith that she was pregnant, his suspicions were suitably riled enough to demand proof. Keith left her at this point, refusing to talk to her until the baby underwent blood tests. Moving in with a retired military veteran with multiple sclerosis and an expert cribbage habit, he took on a position as a care provider. For a while, Keith found himself to be somewhat useful and felt good about what he was doing. This emotion soon turned to pity, however, and Keith began to entertain thoughts about killing the man and putting him out of his misery. Deciding that it was too dangerous to stay around the man lest he be accused of eventual murder, Keith went back to Peggy one final time.

The relationship was more fraught than ever. The couple was living with Peggy's mother, though Keith could go days and weeks without hearing from Peggy. Instead, he would just hear stories about her exploits from fellow truck drivers, about the various liaisons she was having with other men up and down the country.

For the first time in his life, Keith found himself without a job for an extended period of time. He spent his days watching television and going to bars. He began to have ideas, fantasies, and daydreams of a vicious and nasty nature. With the relationship with Peggy heading inevitably towards doom,

Keith found himself needing a new outlet for his emotions. His next move would be the final step into the world of mass murder. After a troubled childhood, a difficult adolescence, and a complicated adulthood, Keith Hunter Jesperson would take his first steps towards becoming a serial killer.

Taunja Bennett

Life for Keith Jesperson was complicated. With work harder to come by, any job seemed like the right one, while his home life had been devastated. The wife and kids had moved far away, and the relationship with Peggy was oscillating wildly between furious arguments and wild, lustful reconciliations. To Keith, it felt as though everything that could be going wrong in his life was going wrong. Even the house he was living in with Peggy felt old and haunted, as though he couldn't stay a day longer. He found himself tired, depressed, and with no easy way out.

This had been made especially difficult by the arrival of the Christmas season. Still a dedicated father, Keith had sold the majority of his possessions in order to be able to afford presents for his kids. His truck, his fishing rod, and his childhood toys had all been sold. Amid this, Keith received a phone call while he was staying at Peggy's mother's house. Peggy was out on the road and placed a collect call to Keith to inform him that she had met a new man while trucking and that he was to move out immediately.

Keith was furious. Falling back on old habits, he wandered out into the street. A stray cat was walking by, until Keith cornered it and wrapped his hands around its throat. Choking the life out of the animal relieved some of the anger.

Moving out of the house, Keith began to miss Peggy. Their relationship was far from ideal, but at least it gave a release to some of the sexual tension Keith felt building up inside himself every day. He was still living in Peggy's house while she was away, with her mother and the ghosts of two men who had reportedly hanged themselves in the home half a century ago.

On the morning of the 21st of January, 1990, Keith left the home. He purposefully only took a couple of dollars with him, worried about overspending in his current financial dire straits. As usual, he wandered from place to place, killing time. Visiting a bar, he played some pool for a while (he was very good) and won a bit of money. This cash was taken to a nearby bar, and by 2pm, Keith had started drinking. The establishment was run down and seedy. Playing pool again (and drinking black coffee), Keith noticed a girl on the other side of the room. She was playing pool with a couple of male friends. She was about a foot shorter than Keith, wore her dark her at shoulder length, and looked a little like a slimmer, prettier version of Rose. The girl smiled effortlessly and seemingly without a care in the world.

When the girl noticed that Keith was staring at her from across the bar, she ran right over and gave him a hug. The confused bartender asked why, to which the girl gave no real answer. Asking later, Keith discovered that she was a girl who hung out with many of the bar's less fortunate, run-down customers. Despite her warmth and pleasant character, it was

46

generally accepted that she was far from the brightest girl. Eventually, she asked Keith to join her and her friends in a game of pool and introduced herself as Taunja. Keith took one look at the lack of money on the table. This usually meant one thing. The girl was feigning interest in order to encourage a confused man into buying her beer. Keith left for home.

At home, Keith found little of interest. Television was dull, and there was little on. Everything seemed to be depressing, and he just couldn't shake the image of the girl from the bar out of his mind. His fantasies ran wild thinking about her. Jumping in his truck, he drove back to see if she was still there.

Just as he pulled the truck up in front of the bar, Taunja was walking out. Keith followed her all the way to the parking lot, thinking that he might be able to convince her to get in his car, and that he might be able to seduce her. Even if she wasn't entirely willing, Keith supposed, he might take her anyway. By this point, she was playing on his mind enough that rational thought was moving further and further into the rear-view mirror.

But it seemed the girl remembered him. Walking up to her and starting a conversation, Taunja smiled while she chatted. Keith invited her to have something to eat, after which they might play a little pool somewhere. To his relief, she accepted. Once she hopped in his car, however, he pulled open his empty wallet. Despite the lack of money on him,

Keith was certain he had a twenty dollar bill left at home. Would she mind if they went back and collected it?

Arriving at the house belonging to Peggy's mother, Keith invited the girl inside. Again, she agreed, but chose to leave behind a few of her possessions (a purse and a Walkman) in the truck. At this point, Keith considered actually taking the girl to a restaurant. His mind was on fire with the possibilities that lay ahead. The idea of treating her well was compelling, but thoughts about what he had done to the stray cat were also beginning to creep into his mental space. Welcoming her inside, Keith closed the door behind them and stepped into the bedroom while he planned his next move.

Keith, caught up in the moment, wasn't sure what he should do. There were fantasies of kidnapping the girl and keeping her as a sexual slave. There was the idea of taking her to dinner and showing her a good time. Exercising total possession over this attractive young girl was appealing, the opposite of what he had had when he was with Peggy. He could keep her under his control for a few weeks before kicking her out of the house. At the back of his mind, he could recall stories about the serial killer Ted Bundy who had done something similar. Some, he remembered thinking at the time, just had it coming.

But as the two stood in the room, Taunja began to interrupt Keith's thought pattern. She asked about the mattress lying on the floor and above the picture of Jesus hanging on the wall. As he explained to her how he would fall asleep on the mattress while watching TV, Keith was fascinating by how much this girl trusted him. Was it because she had been drinking all day? Keith realized that he had total control of the situation.

Thinking this, he walked up behind the girl and kissed her on the back of the neck. Wriggling free, Taunja ran straight for the door. Keith grabbed her before she could run outside. Asking her whether this meant that sex was totally out of the question and receiving no answer, he picked her up and laid her down on the mattress. To all intents and purposes, with the windows curtained and the door shut, she was trapped. Writhing free once again and running to the door, this started to dawn on the girl. Keith wrestled her back onto the mattress, surprised by her resilient strength. She was trembling. Assuming her to be utterly in terror, Keith was shocked when she kissed him. Hurry up, she whispered.

Keith began to have sex with her, feeling her beginning to accept him slowly. While he raped her, she urged him to hurry up. She wanted to get it over with, but this did not please Keith. As he remembers it, he suddenly saw red. As he lay there with her, he began to bring to mind all of the terrible thoughts he'd had about women during his life. For a short time, she seemed to look exactly like Rose.

Swinging a punch, Keith wanted to knock her out with a single blow. But it wasn't enough. He hit her first in the temple. She was still conscious. Again he hit her, but she just stared back blankly. Keith, a former boxer, couldn't understand why this girl would not just fall down unconscious. In the ring, he had been able to knock down men with one punch. Again and again he hit her in the head. This wasn't like the TV. It reminded him of the cats he would kill, but it felt somehow better. This was the first time in his life he had hit a woman in anger, and it felt good. Twenty times he hit Taunja, smashing her features until she was unrecognizable. But she still wasn't unconscious. Despite her battered face, the girl reached up, pulling at the blankets, calling out for her mother to stop the man from hitting her.

Keith found himself torn. What was he going to do next? Meditating on the idea of hogtying the girl to keep her around for sexual purposes, he began to realize that she was not far from death. He could take her to the hospital, leave her like this, or put her out of her misery. The first option was sure to end in jail. He chose the latter.

With his hands around her throat, Keith Jesperson did not stop choking until his knuckles had turned white. Even when he loosened his grip ever so slightly, she was still breathing. Keith continued. This was much harder than killing cats. The girl urinated herself, struggled, and then finally stopped moving. Keith, at last, got off the body, strolled down to the kitchen and poured himself a cup of black coffee. Sitting at the kitchen table, he mulled over what he should do next.

His first move was to get Taunja dressed again. Blood splatters littered the walls and floor; they had to be cleaned up. Looking at the girl's clothes, Keith wondered whether the metal button on her jeans would hold a fingerprint. He cut it off with a steak knife. He washed and dried his own clothes before putting them back on, before making extra sure that his victim was dead by taking a length of nylon rope and tying it tight around her neck. All the while, he shouted at the ghosts in the house that they now had one more for company. Sitting with the body, Keith was caught between enjoying the domineering sense of power and regretfully wishing he could bring her back to life.

This was abandoned when he realized he would need to get to work to rid himself of the body, set up an alibi, and make sure that he could not be caught in the same way as the criminals on the TV shows he watched, such as Perry Mason. Leaving the body behind, he drove back to the back and began to lay the foundations. Drinking beer and chatting till late in the evening, Keith made sure people saw his solitary exit from the building. Afterwards, he drove ten miles out of town to look for a good place to dispose of a body. On the drive home, he made sure he had a full tank of gas and that there were no issues with his headlights that might prompt him being pulled over by the police. He tried to leave nothing to chance, not when he would be transporting a dead girl around.

As he arrived back at the home, he found Taunja still lying there. Feeling woozy while he prepped his exit, he was shocked to hear the phone ring. It was Peggy. They chatted, and it seemed as though Peggy wanted to come home. Staring at the body as he talked, Keith agreed to see her again. As he talked to Peggy, he began to feel sexually stimulated. Staring at the body, he was soon lying next to it, touching the various areas of skin. For years, she would be Keith's favorite fantasy as he remembered the first woman he killed.

By the time he was done, it was after midnight. Rigor mortis had struck the body, and it was difficult to move. Keith dragged her by the rope around her neck. Bundling her into the car, Taunja's head rested against the passenger side window, and it looked as though she was sleeping or drunk. Driving her out into the middle of nowhere, he searched for somewhere to dump the body. New shoes were bought on the way home in case the police could trace the tread of his cycling trainers. As he drove, extra care was taken to stay under the speed limit and not to run any red light. Eventually, a ravine was found about sixty feet from the road. Though he considered covering the body with leaves, Keith was worried he had seen a car approaching and ran away. He drove away quickly, worried that he'd left the girl too exposed.

Taunja's Walkman was thrown onto a road to be run over by traffic, en route to a small truck stop Keith intended to visit. As he sat and drank coffee in the diner, three policemen walked in. Paranoid, Keith seized upon the opportunity to build up his alibi. Thoughts raced back to the girl's purse, which was still in the car. Staying at the truck stop until 8 in the morning, Keith made sure that he was seen by plenty of people. He then drove three miles away and hurled the purse into the center of a blackberry thicket.

Arriving back at the house, he opened a few windows to deal with the smell and cleaned, scraped, and washed the blood from the walls. Sheets and blankets were cleaned, and the floor was vacuumed. Keith even steam-cleaned the carpet. The next few days were spent hastily adding to as many alibis as possible, while worrying about anyone finding out what he'd done. Thoughts of suicide popped across Keith's mind while the girl's face was constantly at the forefront of his thoughts.

Several days later, reports emerged that a biker had found the body. The newspaper seemed to suggest that the police were searching for the two men who had been seen playing pool with Taunja in the bar. Suicidal thoughts were abandoned – it would bring too much shame on the family – but guilty thoughts persisted. Soon these ideas turned to acceptance and then regret that Keith hadn't managed to keep her alive a short while and abused her at his whim. But for now, it seemed as though Keith Jesperson had gotten away with murder.

Claudia

A short time later, Keith read in the paper that two people had been charged with the murder of Taunja Bennett. But rather than her drinking companions, it emerged that a couple Keith described as "barflies" had been arrested instead. The woman had confessed to carrying out the murder with her boyfriend, and this had been enough to convict, especially when the girl had driven the police out to the exact spot where the body was dumped. But as weird as it was, Keith was not going to change anybody's mind. He let the two take the blame for the murder.

Meanwhile Peggy arrived home with her two kids in tow. She went back to waitressing, having abandoned truck driving as too much hard work. Keith was left at home to take care of the kids. The relationship with Peggy was breaking down. Often Keith would wake up in the middle of the night with his hands around her neck. The thoughts of the murdered girl loomed large, and he realized that he would need to get away from the haunted house before he went mad.

Two months after his first murder, Keith moved south. During the drive to Sacramento, thoughts about killing played through his mind. Trying to drive them out, he considered women who he had met during his trucking jobs, considering what they might be up to these days. One in particular, Nancy, occupied his thoughts enough that he decided to pay her a visit. Finding no one at home, he went to a local diner to learn that she had been raped and killed by two men who were now in jail. A shame, Keith thought, as he might have been able to kill her himself.

Back on the road, Keith began to think about the female hitchhikers who were usually trying to pick up a lift at truck stops. A chance encounter with a woman named Jean saw him drive the pair (including Jean's baby) out to a secluded spot. After forcing her into oral sex, Keith's mind ran hot with the idea of murder before he realized he'd have to kill the baby as well. He stepped out of the car and allowed himself to calm down. Jean attempted to run away with the child, but he managed to convince her to allow him to drive her back into town. She agreed, and they set off. Looking back on the incident, Keith was worried. The woman had his name, his destination, and the details of how he'd assaulted her. Chasing the thoughts from his mind, he went back out on to the road.

The incident prompted police interest. Arriving at a hotel, Keith found himself surrounded by cops. He tried to play off the story as a simple misunderstanding, telling the police he regretted having sex with a married woman. If he had wanted to hurt her, he suggested, why would he have let her get away, or why would he have driven her back into town? The cops seemed convinced, but fingerprinted him anyway and told him to check in with a detective back in the town. Keith did exactly this, feeding the detective the same story. Not once did he mention how he had been so sorely tempted to break the woman's neck. The story seemed to be enough, and Keith drove off to attend his new construction job.

The job lasted two months, all spent with the prospect of further recrimination hanging over Keith's head from the police. Once it finished, he headed back to Portland and reconciled with Peggy. But an incident with his and Rose's son, Jason, quickly meant that Keith saw no other option than to move back closer to his original family. With Peggy and her kids in tow, Keith took a trucking job nearer Rose and the kids and hit the road once again, Peggy joining him for the ride. Although it had seemed ideal when viewed through rose-tinted lenses, Keith was soon exhausted and annoyed again. But a stroke of luck saw the couple who had been arrested for Taunja's murder convicted. The woman had changed her plea at the last minute, saying she had just wanted to annoy her boyfriend. However, the process was already too far along. In order to avoid the chance of the death penalty, the couple pleaded guilty and received 15 years to life.

Things didn't continue to be quite so peachy, however. Pulled over for a minor trucking issue, Keith was nearly extradited back to California on charges of sexual assault. When he was being arrested, he told Peggy about how he had killed a girl, though mentioned no names. The charges were eventually reduced, after spending a few nights in the cells, and Keith's trucking company sent him money to catch a bus home. Sitting in one bus stop waiting for a ride, Keith ventured into the toilets. He took out a pen and wrote on the wall. In his

57

piece of graffiti, he confessed to the murder of Taunja Bennett, gave a time and place, mentioned that he had killed and raped the girl, and that he had enjoyed it. The message finished with the proclamation that despite the other people taking the blame, the real killer was still free. He signed the message with a smiley face, summing up the cocky, arrogant attitude he had hoped to convey. Two months later, after nothing had come of the message, Keith did the same in another restroom, this time including the detail about cutting off the button of the girl's jeans. The cops, he thought, must be genuinely too stupid to catch him.

Keith bounced around various jobs but still harbored fantasies about the girl he'd killed. Thoughts of rape led to close calls for a number of women, when Keith abstained at the last minute from pouncing on them in the dark, while he began to solicit prostitutes and, in his own words, "treated them rough." One of these girls fought back and pepper-sprayed him in the face. Despite almost two years passing since his first murder, the thoughts of the second were never far away.

During the hot summer of 1992, these fantasies crept back into his mind. Working on the mechanics of the truck in one stop, Keith was surprised to find a woman introducing herself to him, asking for a ride. She said her name was Claudia, that she wanted a ride to Los Angeles, and that she had been hitching lifts with truckers. To Keith, she wasn't beautiful, but she was "pretty enough." As she was getting into the truck, his mind was already racing with criminal thoughts.

The two spent a short time on the road together before Keith stopped, leaned over, and kissed Claudia. Feeling a lack of returned affection, he sat back to be told that, if he wanted sex, he need only ask. There were set prices for these things. Informing the passenger that he never paid for sex, Keith again pressed against the girl. She still refused, but the moment had taken him, and he instantly starting ripping her clothes off and forcing himself upon her, again and again.

Eventually Keith stopped and drove a little way for lunch. Despite raping her, Claudia didn't run away from Keith as soon as possible. Instead, she asked him for some drugs. When she was informed that he never touched narcotics, she jumped on the CB radio and began to ask any truckers in the area for heroin. Snatching the microphone from her, Keith pressed a twenty dollar bill into her hand. She would not starve in his truck, but he would not tolerate drugs of any kind. Claudia demanded more, threatened to tell a security guard how Keith had forced himself on her. Keith locked the doors.

There was a roll of duct tape hidden beneath his seat, and he grabbed it. Both her arms were taped together in front of her while her ankles received the same treatment. Checking to see if there was anyone else in the parking lot, Keith punched the girl in the side of the neck. She fell unconscious.

Now fully accepting that he was about to murder his second victim, Keith resolved to do a better job of it this time. Taping her to the bed, he decided to rape Claudia again. As he was

59

doing so, a police unit pulled up in the parking lot. They had a dog with them. Parking their car in the shade of Keith's truck, the men went to eat in the diner while the dog cooled down in the car. Starting the truck, Keith pulled out ever so slowly and joined back onto the interstate.

As he was driving along, Claudia was in the back trying to free herself. Unfastened from the bed, she was free of the tape and getting dressed. Braking suddenly, Keith pounced on her and tied the girl down once again. At the next stop, he raped her again. And so he started a lethal game, choking the girl until she was unconscious and then allowing her to breathe again. This happened two, three, four times, again and again and again. When she finally died, Keith pulled to the side of the road, drank an ice tea, and tried to figure out how to dispose of the body.

In the shade of the San Bernardino Mountains, Keith scouted out a deep ravine. He fell asleep, waiting until darkness fell, with only a blanket between him and the dead girl. Waking up around 7 in the evening, the CB radio was alive with truckers talking about a police car parked in front of a truck matching Keith's description. Jumping out, he chatted with the officer and pretended to be concerned about his tires. Satisfied that the cop thought everything was in order, Keith and the corpse pulled out on to the highway and drove some distance.

Over ten miles away, just off Highway 95, Keith pulled over and dragged the corpse into a canyon. Hidden by bushes and taking care to cover the girl with tumbleweed, he was satisfied that she would not be found nearly as quickly. He washed his sleeping bag to rid it of the smell of the dead girl and dried it in the truck's windjammer. To him, Claudia had deserved to die. Having now committed two murders (nearly three) and gotten away with it, Keith was beginning to feel untouchable. The journey was completed as per the schedule, and Keith spent his days thinking about how easy it was to murder.

Cynthia Lyn Rose

Now, Keith had double the murder fantasies. Thoughts of killing both Taunja and Claudia rifled through his mind. Murder and rape became an obsession. But this new lust wasn't matched by his latest driving assignment. The truck itself and the long hours left him feeling tired and despondent when, pulling into a rest area in California a month later, he met a young girl named Cynthia who asked him whether he wanted to party.

Keith fondled a breast beneath the girl's sweatshirt (his method of guarding against potential police sting operations) but declined. She was either in her late twenties or in her early thirties, he couldn't tell. Saying her name was Cynthia, she pressed the matter. But Keith insisted that he was tired. He might be in the mood later, he told the girl, but right now he just wanted to sleep. He shut down the truck, turning off the light to dissuade any further advances. Thoughts on his mind of violent prostitutes in Florida were recalled, when one woman had started killing truckers she picked up in parking lots.

Just as he was lying down to sleep, the passenger door jolted open, and Cynthia jumped in. Keith was furious. Reaching out and grabbing her neck, he dragged her on to the bed and started choking the life out of her. She went limp soon after, and he realized the girl wasn't conscious. Keith Jesperson's third victim was already dead, and all he could feel was regret that he'd missed the chance to play his death games with her. They hadn't even had sex.

Worried that he was being watched, Keith decided that he needed to leave. He drove the truck away fast, driving barefoot. Still driving, the thought occurred to him that Cynthia might wake up, just like Claudia had done. He stopped the truck, and despite all signs pointing toward the girl being dead, he bound and gagged her anyway. Just then, he heard someone breathing. She was still alive.

Content that the bindings would hold her in place, Keith drove on. The aim was to reach the weigh station a few miles away, hoping to provide a convincing alibi of his whereabouts at the time the girl went missing. It was closed when he arrived. Pulling into the parking lot of a nearby café instead, he began to suspect that the cabin was smelling like death. She might have been dead after all.

Once the truck was parked, he jumped into the cabin to check what was happening. Cynthia was a pretty girl. The bed was wet with her urine. There was no indication as to why she had just jumped into his truck. But now here she was. Dead. There was a tree in the corner of the parking lot, one with weeds and garbage at the base. Dumping the body here would keep it hidden for a while. Ripping the duct tape from her wrists, Keith was worried about other truckers arriving. He flung the body onto the garbage, covering her with tumbleweed as a kind of gravestone.

Paranoia was still reigning in his thoughts, and Keith had to drive fast. He needed to get away from the body and the parking lot where Cynthia had last been spotted. During a brief stop, he cleaned the mattress and threw the sheets away. He tried to catch a bit of sleep in the parking lot of a diner. The act of killing itself didn't bother Keith anymore, but the fear of being caught was very real.

The next week was spent checking every detail of every parking lot. Wherever Keith stopped, he was worried about police attention. In restaurants, he would eat with his back to the wall, watching all the time. After a few weeks glued to the CB radio in fear, it seemed as though nothing was being said. Keith had gotten away with it once again. By this time, the couple who had been imprisoned for Taunja's murder were serving their third year. Keith was on to his third victim. The fear of repercussions, whether legal or religious, stopped being an issue. Keith Jesperson feared no one.

Laurie Ann Pentland

November, 1992 saw Keith driving up the Pacific coast, heading eventually towards Salem. With a truckload of meat to deliver, his mind was occupied by the thoughts of companionship. Arriving at a truck stop in Wilsonville, he remembered that he had known a prostitute in the area who went by the name of Laurie. To his recollection, the girl was in her early twenties, and despite not being the most beautiful, certainly knew how to show him a good time. The last three stops in Wilsonville had involved a visit from Laurie, though each time she had raised the price she charged. Keith began to wonder about her whereabouts and put out a message on the radio, but it was still early.

An hour later, he heard Laurie's voice calling out over the airwaves. Replying, he told her where to find him. Just as before, he price had gone up five dollars, she informed him upon arrival at the truck. Keith accepted and paid the girl, spending the next hour having sex. As she began to get dressed before leaving to search for another client, Keith got talking to her. She began to insist that Keith owed her an extra forty dollars, having taken up an hour of her time where most men were satisfied with just a quarter of that. The two began to quarrel over the amount, Keith insistent that they'd had a deal. Soon, Laurie was threatening to call the cops. Flatly, Keith informed her that she had no idea about the risk she was taking. Still she argued, insisting on being paid the extra money.

Keith took hold of Laurie and thrust her down on the bed. Taking her throat in his hands, he began to choke her to death. Just before she was completely out of breath, Keith relented. He allowed her to come back to consciousness before choking her again. This was repeated for an hour, with the killer watching and later remembering how Laurie's will to live flickered and eventually died right in front of him. When she closed her eyes for the last time, Keith kept choking until he was sure she had died. Shutting the body up in the cabin, he went into the diner for a cup of coffee.

Drinking his coffee, Keith mulled over what he considered to be the stupidity of the truck stop prostitutes, these women who so willingly put themselves in harm's way. Finished, he walked back to his vehicle and began to grope the body. Inside her pockets was close to $250. Already Keith's thoughts were wandering to how best to dispose of the body. He focused on a little parking lot not far from his final drop off, a place where he could cover her with vines and garbage containers.

The route he took when heading south was determined by which authorities would give him the least bother. While not the most direct course, Keith was at least sure that this would keep him away from cops. By the time he arrived in the parking lot, it was two in the morning. There was not only an abundance of foliage and garbage to hide the body, there was a six-foot fence bordering the property to provide extra cover. The place was empty.

Laurie was dragged out of the cabin by her hair. The body fell to the ground with a dull thud before being dragged to the fence and covered with leaves, junk, and anything else. Satisfied, Keith left the corpse, drove some hundred yards down the road to a nearby Waremart, and slept in the parking lot, ready to deliver the truck's load in the morning.

The next day, Keith's first thoughts were to blame the girl for her own death. If only she hadn't insisted on being paid that little bit extra. Next, he realized that he would have to stop killing soon. One of these days, he was bound to get caught. Murder was almost too easy for him as a trucker. But if he wanted to be sure of stopping, he might have to give up life on the road. Maybe he didn't even know how to stop these murders.

Cindy

It was another four months before Keith Jesperson found himself on the brink of murder. At the time, he was out on a job, driving south on the I-5. It was a cool, rainy evening in March. He made the decision to pull into a diner in California for some refreshment. The police, to this point, were none the wiser about the various killings. There was not even any suggestion that they had been linked at all. Aside from the first murder, which had already seen a conviction, the others were scattered across the country, the bodies dumped where they had been difficult to find. All this time, Keith had continued to crisscross the country, driving wherever he pleased. No one questioned why a trucker might be travelling so far, so frequently. It was almost the perfect cover story, a fact which was incredibly prevalent in Keith's mind. As he arrived at the truck stop, he wiped the rain droplets from his trousers and spotted the thick fog rolling in off the wide ocean. Not wanting to stop long, he decided to leave the engine idling while he stepped inside. This way, the cab would keep its heat for the journey ahead.

Inside was busy. People seemed to have rushed inside to escape the wet and the cold. As ever, Keith was watching his weight, determined to keep any fat from his hefty frame. This meant a diet heavy on Slim Fast, but a craving for fruit meant a change. Despite the crowds, one girl in the truck stop caught his eye. She was wet from the rain, like most of the other clientele, and seemed to just be sitting and staring at her food. Sipping a hot mug of coffee, she seemed to be half starved. To Keith, she seemed like something of a drifter, someone who almost certainly was spending some time on the streets for whatever reason. Her long hair and thick glasses hid a lot of the scarlet complexion from the rest of the world, but Keith had the instinct that she was hoping to score her dinner from someone.

In that instant, Keith Jesperson decided that he would need to have this woman. She reminded him a little of his schoolteachers, of other motherly women who had scolded him. These considerations were pushed out of his mind as he focused on his sudden urges. Thanks to his career as a truck driver, he felt, he was once again presented with the perfect opportunity to exercise his most base desires. Summoning the waitress, he pointed out the sodden girl and told the waitress that anything the girl wanted to eat, he was happy to cover the cost. Don't tell her who bought the food, Keith informed the serving girl, as the last thing he wanted was someone to start following him around hoping for more. In reality, he just hoped that the waitress wouldn't be able to make the connections between the two clients should the police come to call.

The girl ate, and Keith watched her. Looking up at one point, the hungry youngster seemed to offer a thankful glance in Keith's direction, seemingly aware that he was her mysterious benefactor. Motioning her over, she stood up and then sat down again, this time in front of the trucker. And then she talked. Keith let her talk, while she explained her name was Cindy. She tried to pry more information about the man sitting opposite her. Ducking all of the big or personal questions, he let her talk, aware that all the girl probably wanted was a warm, dry bed for the night. Keith was more than happy to oblige.

As time rolled on, conversation turned to where Keith was heading. Revealing that he was heading for Salinas, Cindy begged him to take her along. Drop her in Sacramento, she pleaded, where there was a sister who could offer her somewhere to stay. After Keith played coy, the girl began to beg. This sealed her fate in the killer's eyes. He hated when they begged. All women, Keith thought, seemingly just wanted something from him. He agreed to give her a lift. By the time he had paid for the meals and picked up some orange juice for the trip, the girl was already waiting outside the cabin. Everything she owned was with her, and it wasn't much.

On the road, Keith turned up the heat in the cabin to give her a chance to dry her hair. It also had the side effect of encouraging her to take off her heavy rain coat, allowing him to get a better idea of the body beneath. After the pair stopped in a gas station to use the restroom, Keith could tell that she had spent a little bit longer inside than she needed. Cindy was now wearing makeup, had combed her hair, and had undone the top three buttons on her blouse. They made one more stop and, returning to the cabin, Keith reached over and kissed his passenger. This time, his victim kissed back. Moving back into the bunk, the two had sex for the next few hours.

It was so warm in the cabin, Cindy suggested to Keith as they lay next to one another that they just spend the night there. Keith assured her that they would, though added that she probably wouldn't enjoy herself. Sitting up, the girl asked him what he meant. It meant, Keith revealed, that he was going to kill her. She could only seem to stare back in disbelief. He raped her once more, easily overpowering the smaller victim. Once again, he played his game whereupon he choked the girl until she lost consciousness, allowed her to wake up, and then choked her again. She only lasted five times before she was strangled to death.

By this time, Keith Jesperson was well aware of what he needed to do next. He still thought long and hard about how best to dispose of the body. First, he put Cindy's clothes back on her body and placed her next to the cabin door. Travelling as he was across the country, hiding the body wasn't even that essential. Thanks to the nature of interstate and even intercounty investigations, especially concerning the types of girls who were normally Keith's prey, the threat of investigation was minimal. However, he didn't know this yet. He still spent a good amount of time picking out the right spot, hiding her body, and then covering it in rocks and vegetation. By the time he reached his destination and dropped off the load on the back of the truck, the rain had cleared.

Susanne

In the six months following the murder of the woman known as Cindy, Keith Jesperson avoided killing. By the time 1993 reached the autumn months, however, the feeling and the urge to kill was again creeping up in Keith's mind. At this point, he confessed his actions to a friend, seeking advice on how to stop murdering women. But the friend, after dismissing the subject as a joke, soon didn't want to talk about it anymore. He advised Keith to see a psychologist and ceased to take part in the conversation. Keith lost a potential outlet on his murderous urges.

Fast forward a few months later, and Keith was sitting in a truck stop in Oregon, drinking coffee and watching the world go by. As he sat and watched, a short blonde woman entered the room. The woman sat down in front of Keith, facing away from him in the next booth. Speaking out loud, Keith said that she had a back he would like to rub. The girl laughed and welcomed him over to the table.

She said her name was Julie, Julie Winningham. Struck by Keith's six foot six frame, she wondered where exactly he'd come from. The two spent the next couple of hours chatting and discovered they were very much attuned to one another's sensibilities. Feeling she was a few classes of respectability above most of the women he met in truck stops, Keith invited her along on his trip and promised that there would be no funny business. It was totally down to her, he assured, her choice entirely. She was given free rein to fall in love with him, but it would always be her decision. Julie accepted the invitation, left a little note in her car window assuring any readers that she'd be away for a while and then hopped into the cabin.

Their first stop was Seattle, after which they headed to Yakima. Everywhere they went, people seemed to love Julie. Keith's friends along his regular routes all commented on the short blonde woman he had in tow. The next stop involved hauling potatoes to Irvine, California. Starting Friday night, they had to be there by Sunday morning. Keith decided to drive all night and made it just after midnight on the Saturday. This gave the pair of them a free day, which they spent at a fairground. Keith even bought Julie a necklace and a bracelet. The only bone of contention reared its head when Julie seemed annoyed that her new friend swore off drugs of any type.

Regardless, they spent the night partying together and wound up having sex in Keith's truck, though he confessed that it wasn't the best or most exciting intimate experience he'd ever had. After spending money on jewelry and a night out, he had hoped for a bit more effort on her part. A quick trip to the phone booth to check in with his employers meant that Keith left Julie alone in the truck. By the time he got back, he discovered that she was trying to use the CB radio to try and pick up drugs.

The couple settled into more romantic concerns before Julie asked Keith whether he'd like to marry her. Unknown to the trucker at the time, she was on the lookout for someone to take good care of her, and it seemed as though Keith fit the bill. He agreed, and despite lambasting her for trying to score drugs over the radio, ventured out to buy some marijuana from one of the other drivers at the truck stop. The two spent a few more nights together before Keith drove her back to the place where she had left her car, and the two parted ways.

After that, it became a regular feature of Keith's trips that he would call in and see Julie whenever he passed. She ended up renting a room with his friends, Ginny and Billy Smith. The arrangement worked for almost twelve months before Keith grew suspicious of both Billy and Julie's intentions. While he suspected his friend of being attracted to his girl, he suspected Julie of simply using him for a ride, for cash, and for drugs. He decided to ditch her after almost a year of dating. In Keith's opinion, she was more in love with marijuana than him.

Just after he dumped Julie, Keith came across an article detailing the case of the two "barflies" who had been convicted of the murder of Taunja Bennett. It annoyed him. The messages he had left scrawled on the restroom walls had failed to have any kind of impact. To rectify this and take back a bit of credit, Keith decided to write a note to the Washington County Courthouse. The note detailed not only where the body had been placed, but the exact wounds, the way she had been tied, where the Walkman and the purse had been thrown away, the buttons cut off from the jeans, and the position she had been left in after he had raped her. Again, he signed the note with a smiley face. In the weeks afterwards, there was no mention in the papers. While his instinct told him to leave the matter alone, Keith couldn't help remain curious about what was happening behind the scenes.

In April of 1994, he wrote another note. It had been four years since the first murder. This note contained a first page with the same old Happy Face logo emblazoned across the front. Rather than sending it to the authorities, however, Keith decided that he might get better results by sending it to the press. As well as Taunja, the note explained how he had killed the girl, as well as hinting as to why he might have done it, and that she was not his only victim. This note failed as well, so a follow-up letter was composed and delivered to the same paper. This time, he talked of his latest murder, as well as his life as a long haul trucker. The note informed people of where the body had been left and just how easy it was to get away with all of these killings. There was even a hint that the writer of the note wanted to stop the murders but just didn't know how. Signing off with confirmation that he was the same man who had sent the last letter, he warned the reader to "check over your shoulder."

At the bottom of each communication, whether it was on the wall of a restroom or the blue paper Keith used to send to the newspaper, he always left a signature Happy Face logo.

During this period, Keith was desperate to know what was going on inside his own head. He began to read through a lot of magazines and books on the subject of serial killers. On one occasion, on opening a magazine dedicated to the subject, he found an article asking whether there was another serial killer on the loose in Oregon. It was about him. Finally seeing his deeds in print, Keith wrote in to the magazine and corrected a few points in their article. He even revealed where they might find another body. But there was never a follow-up piece in the publication.

The library was a great source for books on psychology. One such book, written by a former FBI man, gave the childhood warning signs for a serial killer as three-fold. Typically, they would wet their beds, torture animals, and start fires. To Keith's mind, he filled two out of three categories. Accordingly, he wondered whether setting fires out in the wilderness might satiate the urge to kill. He would start fires and then retreat to a safe distant, from which he could watch as the police and fire brigade struggled to deal with the raging inferno in the dry undergrowth. This worked for a while. Keith thought it might even have saved a few lives. Oregon, Washington, California, Arizona, and Nevada were all victims of his arson attacks at one time or another. It was enough to put off murder for almost a year.

The change came near the end of 1994. Keith Jesperson was driving truckloads of aluminum coils to Florida. After dropping off the delivery, he noticed a blonde woman strolling around a store. She reminded him of Taunja, especially in her slightly Slavic features. The girl was looking for a lift north, and Keith offered up his truck. She gave her name as Susanne.

Susanne was somewhere around thirty years old and carried tarot cards with her. She might have been a fortune-teller, Keith thought. The girl hopped in his truck, and the two were set to drive off. Just before they left, she wondered whether they might stop past Miami along the way to Keith's stop in Georgia. The trucker refused, as it would involve a 400 mile trip out of his way. He refused, but she didn't mind. Susanne just wanted to get out of Florida.

The trip was going according to plan, including stops to eat spaghetti in diners, reloading the truck, and setting off back towards the northwest. Susanne even agreed to sleep in the bunk, provided that they both remain dressed for the entire time. Keith agreed, and they drove until three in the morning, when he had to pull over to sleep. There were a few cop cars out front, and the only parking space was next to the lot's security guard. Keith parked there anyway. He climbed into bed with her, fully clothed, and began to fall asleep. As it seemed, choking, rape, and murder were far from his mind.

But the conditions inside the cabin were hot. The air conditioner was broken, and this caused Keith to wake up in the middle of the night sweating. He needed to open a window, anything to deal with the temperature that was getting close to ninety degrees. Turning on the light inside the truck, he couldn't help but notice the shape of his companion's body as she lay in bed. He couldn't help but take off his clothes and slide in right next to her.

Susanne began to stir, and when she was finally awake and realized what was happening, let out a piercing scream. Keith threw the palm of his hand over her mouth. As she struggled, he desperately tried to think how he might explain this to the security guards or the police. Whatever it was this girl told the police, it seemed that every eventuality ended up in Keith losing his job. Riders were strictly forbidden, rapists even more so.

The girl pleaded to be let go, assuring Keith that she wouldn't tell anyone what had happened. Apologizing, he assured her that she only needed to do as he asked. His first request was that she have sex with him, as though they "were lovers." Susanne saw no way out other than to play along. After a few hours together, she seemed relaxed enough to fall asleep ,but Keith was concerned that she might be faking. Becoming aroused again, he lifted her skirt and tried to force his way inside the sleeping girl. Once again, she screamed. This time, he choked her to death.

While the body was still warm, Keith drove away from the truck stop. He hid her body in some bushes along the side of the road. This time, he took the care to tie some lengths of nylon rope around the girl's neck, a calling card should he even need to prove that the murder had been his. Back in the truck, he drove as fast as he could towards the next weigh station, desperate to be noted in the official books as far away from there as possible.

As far as the records went, it seemed like he had never been near the area at all. Once again, Keith Jesperson seemed to have gotten away with murder.

Angela Subrize

A minor accident in January of 1995 meant that Keith was holed up in a hotel in Spokane. After his truck had spontaneously caught fire, he was waiting for a mechanic's report to confirm that he wasn't guilty of error while waiting for his company to give the go-ahead for his next job. While he waited, he sat in the hotel and had a drink. A woman walked into the bar, with long dark hair, pale blue eyes, and a pile of bags. She sat drinking a beer by herself and, soon enough, Keith managed to charm his way into sharing a drink with the girl.

Before she had even checked in, Keith had offered to put her up in his room for the night. She gratefully accepted and said that her name was Angela. Together, they ordered pizza and beer to be sent up to the room. Angela was a strip tease dancer, with a small tattoo of Tweety Bird raising his middle finger to the world. A short talk and a few beers later, the couple spent the night together.

The next day, Keith was awake before his companion. Needing to leave, he placed thirty dollars on the bedside table and a note on how the girl could reach him if she wanted to meet up again. That day, he walked down to the mechanics to find out that he was absolved of guilt for the fire and that his company had a new load ready and waiting to go. A few deliveries later, he checked in with the head office, only to find that a girl named Angela Subrize had been trying to contact him. Keith phoned her and discovered that she was angling for a lift down to Denver. It wasn't on the way, but Keith came to an arrangement whereby he'd pick her up in a few days, and the couple would go together. Angela gave him directions, and the date was set.

They met at Angela's house, and as Keith carried the girl's bags out to his truck, she grabbed hold of his arm and hugged it tight in gratitude. The night they had spent together had pleased Keith, but he still had a long haul of almost 300 miles in the next few hours, so he couldn't think too much about such subjects. They paused to eat at one truck stop and wound up eating alongside a woman named Lady Rose, who ran one of the CB radio stations that truckers turned to for their weather reports. She told Keith that there was snow and ice coming the way he was heading, which would mean a long night ahead with very few miles covered.

The two drove on for the next few days, with Keith driving and Angela sleeping in the back of the cabin. When they pulled to the side of the road, they would find distracting ways of entertaining one another. When they reached Wyoming, Keith overhead his companion arguing in a telephone booth. He had let her use his credit card to make a long distance call, and now it sounded like it wasn't going too well. After speaking with her dad, it seemed that he no longer had any inclination to see her. Instead, she asked Keith whether they could drive to Indiana, where she knew an old boyfriend who might be able to help her out.

By this time, Keith had grown weary of his new passenger. It was clear by this point that she was chiefly interested in him as a means of getting around the country. Now that she had a new man to go to in Indiana, it seemed as though she was someone else's responsibility. They had sex again after Angela got off the phone, but this time – once they were finished – it seemed as though she had started giving orders. Let's go, she told him. Keith didn't take kindly to this sort of instruction. This prompted a long-winded story from Angela about the series of guys who had let her down in the past, culminating in her claim that she believed herself to be pregnant. It was her belief that the baby belonged to the ex-boyfriend in Indiana, though she couldn't be sure. The concept riled Keith, who suggested that she might have even suggested it had been his. He accused Angela of using him as a free ride. They'd both enjoyed themselves, Angela claimed, but now they should get going for Indiana as soon as possible.

With worrying ideas beginning to rise up in his mind, Keith jumped back into the truck with his travel companion and got onto Interstate 80. The roads were thick with snow. While Angela slept in the cabin, Keith's mind ran hot with the ideas of what might happen if the boyfriend in Indiana didn't want to take the girl back. What if he rejected her? What if she claimed the baby belonged to Keith? What if the boyfriend didn't even exist, and she faked the call? Furious, Keith burrowed through the sleeping girl's purse. He found a can of pepper spray and removed it, hiding it where it wouldn't be found.

The weather got worse. They passed a number of jackknifed trucks that were almost wrecked. Visibility fell to just a few feet. There was still two days to go until they reached Indiana, and Keith desperately needed to sleep. They reached a rest area in Nebraska and pulled over. It would take a four- or five-hour lie down until Keith felt up to driving again. But this didn't sit well with Angela. After waking up from the back of the cabin to find that they'd pulled over, she was furious. In a hurry, she wanted to be back on the road instantly and couldn't wait for Keith to sleep. If she wanted to get there quicker, he informed her, she was welcome to get on the radio and beg for a lift.

Angela's mood changed. Instead of anger, she switched into seduction. The pair had sex, though Keith was half asleep. When he finished and rolled over to continue his nap, she went straight back to anger. She wanted to go, and she wanted to go now. Keith didn't care. After he had slept for twenty minutes, she jerked him awake. Angela refused to sit there for one more minute while they were not moving. Turning his back and resuming his sleep, Keith just tried to ignore the girl. This went on for an hour. He'd fall asleep, and just as he was starting to recharge, she'd kick him awake and insist they get back on the road. By this time, the sleepy Keith had already marked her down as a dead girl.

Waking up, Keith started to drive. They drove further through Nebraska until they reached a secluded truck stop with no customers. Stating that he needed to use the restroom, Keith stepped out to make sure that no one was nearby and that there was no traffic passing. There was no one in sight.

Keith climbed back into the cabin and ordered the girl to make the bed. He forced himself upon her, and while she begged him to stop, he pulled out the duct tape. Angela promised to be good, promised to behave. She even started praying for her own safety, her hands clasped in front of her chest, and her words loud enough for Keith to hear. Keith lied to her, saying he'd never hurt her. They had sex again. Afterwards, Angela mentioned that she was hungry and asked to stop at a restaurant. Knowing that this was all it took for her to get out and alert the authorities, Keith laughed it off.

Angela reached for her pepper spray. When Keith accused her of doing so, she tried to plead ignorance. Again, he laughed. And so he reached out his hands and began to choke the girl. Four, five times he allowed her to wake up again before he resumed the throttling. After she had finally stopped breathing, Keith slept for five hours.

When he woke up, the first thing Keith did was put Angela's body in a plastic bag. This time was a little bit different than his earlier murders, as people had seen and would be able to remember him spending time with the dead girl. She'd even used his credit card to call up her boyfriend and father. There might even be a police file on her somewhere, possibly with her finger prints already in the records. This wouldn't be someone he could just dump by the side of the road. He would need to make Angela disappear completely.

But first, he needed to eat. Driving to a McDonald's and ordering a meal for two, he sat in the truck and considered his options. Again, he blamed the girl for her own murder, annoyed that she hadn't been up front with him. Again, he fondled the body, just for once last check over what he had done. Once his food was finished, it was time to go to work.

At three in the morning, just ten days after the fire-related accident that had put him up in the hotel, Keith pulled to the side of the road. The body was already starting to take on the rotten smell that was like nothing else in the world. He had grown used to the distinct aroma and knew that it was incriminating. Taking his duct tape, Keith repositioned the girl's hands so that they were stuck out in front of her body. Rigor mortis was already making this a difficult task, so he laid the corpse out along the ground to make it easier. With a length of thick black rope, he fastened the body beneath the truck's trailer. It had just enough give that the body would be able to drag between the wheels, grazing against the tarmac. Fixing her ankles to the underside of the trailer and with her nose almost touching on the road, Keith would be able to grind Angela's face and fingerprints away. She would be unrecognizable.

Next, he waited for a break in the traffic. Putting about three miles between himself and a convoy of truckers, he moved out onto the road. Travelling at around seventy miles an hour, he dragged the body for about twelve miles at top speed before pulling over to check out his handiwork. Looking on the underside of the vehicle, he examined the dead girl. A shoulder was missing, as was a thigh. The chest had been completely smashed, while her intestines, arms, and hands were left strewn somewhere back down the road. The arms were worn away so badly that she only had her shoulders left. To the other truckers on the road, the body pieces must have appeared as just regular road kill.

Dragging the tattered remains out from under the truck and down into a secluded bank, Keith left Angela in the tall grass about fifty feet from the roadside. Trucks were passing, asking whether he needed any help. Keith laughed them off, suggesting that he was just taking a moment to "get rid of [his] coffee." They drove on by. Next, Keith plotted out his route. Phoning into his company and providing a false itinerary, he drove all night to provide himself with a cover story that placed him nowhere near the body. If anyone were to look at the records, Keith Jesperson would apparently have been in an entirely different state.

Julie Ann Winningham

Life after the death of Angela was tough for Keith Jesperson. More than once, he considered suicide. Thoughts of crashing his truck into a concrete barrier were only abandoned after Keith realized how his children might react should the truth about his murders ever come to light. At night, he would steer his truck with the lights off, driving by the light of the full moon. He played pranks on other drivers, slashing fuel lines, puncturing tires, and even chaining two trucks together and watching them try to drive away. It seemed as though, despite the suicidal thoughts, he was having altogether too much fun to die.

That was when Julie Winningham came back into his life. It was a chance encounter in Oregon. Keith ran into his ex-girlfriend while walking out of a restroom in a standard truck stop. He immediately went back into the bathroom, worried that he might not want to talk to her. For all the hassle and annoyance she had brought him, he had a rest day ahead and nothing much to do. Keith decided to spark up a conversation, and the two went for coffee.

Over drinks, they apologized to one another. Keith was certain that she hadn't changed, that she was still a "scammer" but he decided to play along. When she said she was out of cigarettes, he told her that he always kept a special pack of her favorite brand in the truck, just in case he ever ran into her. They were barely in the cabin before she started to kiss him.

The two agreed to go out. First, Julie revealed the hot water she was in. She desperately needed $700 to pay a fine and asked Keith for the money. He played along, hoping that he'd be able to get her into bed and never hand over the actual cash. They went out to a bar, played pool, and got drunk. When they were stumbling back to bed, a drunken Julie proposed. Again, Keith agreed to go along with her, assuming he'd renege on the deal later. His head was already filling up with the old fantasies about trapping a woman and holding her as a sex slave.

They drove up to Julie's mother's house and revealed their engagement plans. They left her shocked mother behind and went back to the truck stop. The two spent the evening together, and by the morning, Keith had fallen back in love with Julie. Murderous thoughts were abandoned, and he was back under her spell.

Calling into his company, Keith found himself with a few days off. Now partnered up with Julie, he had something to do. When he woke her up, she revealed more debts hanging over her head. Car repairs were going to cost her $1000. She had drunkenly crashed the vehicle. A court date had been set and fines for the accident could total a further $1500. If she didn't, then she'd end up in jail. Add in lawyers' bills, and she was having to sell her car in order to make everything work. She asked Keith whether he'd be a witness to the sale and whether he'd sign his name to the contract. The idea worried Keith. What if his signature matched up against the Happy Face letters he had been sending out? If he killed Julie one day, they might be able to match up all the handwriting.

They drove to her friend's house to pay a visit. Keith noticed drugs laid out on the table, and soon enough, Julie was inquiring about buying marijuana. Knowing she had no money to pay for it herself, he started walking back to his truck. In no time, she was chasing him out of the house. Despite his refusal to give her any cash, she whisked his wallet from his pocket and took out two twenty-dollar bills. Fuming, Keith sat in the truck for the next few hours while Julie got high with her friends.

It had been arranged that they would go back out to her mother's house the next day to have dinner. Keith made up some excuse to duck out of the evening. He left and went hiking for a few hours, and by the time he got to the house, Julie and her mother were engaged in a shouting match. They left.

Together over the next week, Keith was eventually reminded of exactly how much Julie used to annoy him. Someone had stolen her car keys. Her own mother had called the police on her. The court date for the drunk-driving case was just around the corner. She didn't have any money. She depended on Keith. She wanted to borrow thirty dollars to get a license to work a temporary job. Keith gave her fifty, but as he fully expected, he got no change. To him, it was "one aggravation after another."

Leaving her with some money at a bar, Keith left to play cribbage. He had fallen asleep by the time Julie made it back to the truck. After they had sex, she sparked up a cigarette, leaned back, and explained just how she and her friends had come to the agreement that it was actually Keith's fault that she had lost her car. He owed her $600 for that. Added to this, she revealed a second drunk-driving offence, so those fines would total more than $2000. She would need that money by the next day. As they were now engaged, she explained, they had to help one another out.

But Keith knew what she was after. This wasn't a marriage of love, but rather one of convenience, He felt she just wanted his money. He didn't have $2000, he informed her, and even if he did, he would never hand it over to her. He didn't like her attitude, and he didn't like being depended on for money. Keith told her as much, but Julie did not react well. She had spent the entire night describing to her friends how often he wanted to have sex with her, and how little she satisfied these urges. If he wasn't going to give her the money, then they would back up her story when she went to the cops and claimed to have been raped.

Angry but remaining calm, Keith warned Julie that she had no idea what she was getting herself into. Julie didn't care. Either

94

she'd get paid, or she'd get the cops. She was already screaming pretty loudly as the pair argued in the back of the truck. Balled up in the corner of the cabin, she just looked like all of the other girls Keith had killed. He lunged for her, surprised to find that she reciprocated his attempts to kiss her. This was all part of the game, Keith thought. After they were done, however, his hands wrapped around her throat and began to cut off her breathing. Her eyes, bulging, seemed to be genuinely shocked.

Choking until Julie passed out, Keith reached for the duct tape, bound her hands behind her back, and tied her ankles together. Her mouth was sealed shut with more tape. Climbing into the driver's seat, he began to steer the truck out onto the road. Julie woke up as they braked hard for a stop sign. Attempting to reach the passenger's seat, she could only flop onto the floor. Falling, her head caught against a corner of the seat, and she cut herself. There was soon blood over the floor. Keith reached down and petted her head. Trying to talk through the duct tape, Julie's words were only muffled noises. She was scared enough that she lost control of her bodily functions. Later, Keith would have to clean the carpet.

When they finally stopped, he picked her up and took her into the back of the cabin. Ripping the tape from her face, Keith announced that they were going to be having a kissing contest. Julie would have to show him just how much her life was worth. And she tried. After they had sex again, Julie plead for her life, explaining that she didn't need the money. She had only been kidding. But it wasn't enough. Bluntly, Keith told Julie Winningham that she was about to die.

Removing the tape from her ankles and closing the curtains, Keith ignored Julie's claims that she felt sick. He tied a shirt around her head as a blindfold and began to touch her body wherever he pleased. Once again, he had sex with her as she pleaded for her life. As she lay on the bed blindfolded, Keith began to recount the stories of his murders. Starting with Taunja Bennett, he rattled off dates and names. He told her how he'd dragged one girl along beneath the truck. And then he started to choke her. Julie woke up and was throttled four times, with Keith even tempted to keep her alive until the next night. But he didn't want to push his luck too far. After he had choked her again, Keith hopped out of the truck and began to urinate against a wheel. As he did so, he spotted a sheriff's car coming along the road. Standing by the wheel of his truck, he waved the officer by as the car carried on past him.

It was nearly dawn. If he waited too long, then it would be too busy to dump the body. But she was still alive. Clambering back inside, Julie was whispering to Keith. She told him that she loved him. She assured him that she would never say anything. He touched her hair, kissed her face, and said that everything would be alright. She would be allowed to prove her love. With his encouragement, they fooled around again. After that, Keith strangled her for the final time.

Keith and the body drove down Highway 14. As it happened, they were near the spot where he had dumped Taunja's body all those years ago. Jumping over a fence at the side of the road, he threw the corpse down a fifteen foot slope and watched as the crumpled Julie lay at the bottom of the ravine. By the time he was back in the truck, he had begun to realize just how many people had seen them together. If the authorities came looking, he'd be a prime suspect. Later on that night, Keith decided to sneak back to the roadside and move the body. But he never bothered. Tired of being a serial killer, he felt that this was the best way to get caught. While he would never hand himself in, he knew that they would be coming for him eventually. This time, he had gone too far.

Capture

Despite Julie's death, Keith tried to keep to his normal schedule. He hauled trucks across the country, stopped occasionally to play cribbage, and even hit on some of the girls in the truck stops. One of the girls received a few of Julie's coats as a present, which he instantly knew was a mistake. Nearly forty now, Keith was worried about his soon-to-expire driving license. Whenever he saw a cop, he didn't know whether he'd be asked about murder, an out-of-date license, or anything else.

Over the coming weeks, he felt paranoid. One night, he almost took a girl back to his truck with murderous deeds on his mind, but they kissed and said good night before she clambered inside. Instead, Keith lay back on his bunk and listened to the CB radio, as truckers and prostitutes arranged to meet one another. The urges were becoming overpowering, and feeling like it was too much, he stepped outside and resolved to go for a walk.

Before he could get both feet on the ground, a voice shouted out from behind. It was the security guard who worked at the truck stop. Fully expecting to hear that he was under arrest, Keith paused with baited breath, but it turned out that the man just wanted to chat.

So Keith tried to get back into his regular life. Several times, he had close run-ins with women, but something always got between him and their murder. They might have had a family, or they changed their mind at the last moment. He took to shoplifting detective magazines, just to see if he could. When he came across fellow truckers who worked for the same company, they seemed to try and avoid him. Everything seemed to be on edge, as though something was wrong.

Keith needed some money to cross into New Mexico. He phoned the company, and they agreed to pay it. When the money arrived, he set off. But when he reached the border, the policeman asked for his full name. This never usually happened. They let him pass through, but it seemed as though someone might be wanting to track him. When arriving at the drop off point, the entire crew worked hard to help him unload the truck. Usually, he was stuck doing it himself.

Phoning in to the company offices, he was told that he would need to check again later for his next job. As he drove into two to kill time, a couple of police patrol cars began to follow. Once he was out of town, they overtook him and drove off into the distance. Ringing the company again, he was told there was something for him tomorrow, but in the meantime, he was not to go anywhere. After three days without a load to haul, it seemed odd that they would delay further. Usually, they couldn't turn the truckers round fast enough. Keith was certain they'd been told what to say by the police. Worried and convinced that running away would only prove his guilt, Keith went to bed.

Waking up in the morning, Keith decided to wash his truck. There wasn't much else to do. As he drove up to the wash station, the little "open" light switched off. A man in a black SUV was watching him from the side of the road. Getting on the radio, he inquired as to whether the facility was open. He was told that it was always ready for business. To Keith, this meant that someone didn't want him washing evidence off the truck. Calling through to his trucking company, he finally got his orders. When he asked what the load was going to be, they didn't have an answer. They always had an answer. Possibly machine parts, they told him.

Keith drove up to the pickup site and parked a good distance away. He watched for any clues, but the fairground seemed deserted. Just as he reached the front gate, the same SUV from earlier pulled up alongside his truck. The man jumped out and told Keith that his load was right in the center of the site, and while he didn't have the keys to the front gate, they just had to drive through a gap at the side of the fence.

As he pulled into the site, he noticed how tight the space was. It had been like threading a needle driving in, and that didn't leave him much room to load. But if he drove in, then Keith believed enough in his own abilities to be able to drive out again. Dismounting from the cabin, he followed the man as they went looking for the load.

Two men stepped out from the shadows. Wearing suits and wielding guns, they ordered Keith to face the wall and spread his legs. They checked him for weapons. After he asked just what the hell was going on, he was informed that he was wanted as part of an "ongoing investigation." This told Keith nothing. Arson. Murder. Rape. He could be wanted for a number of crimes. When he was forced into a patrol car, he was reassured by the New Mexico insignia. He hadn't killed anybody in this state. Sure, he'd set a few wildfires, but that was nothing compared to murder. It was only when the car was a few blocks from the sheriff's office that one of the officers revealed that he was wanted in connection with the death of his fiancé, Julie Winningham. The body had been found a day after the murder. Keith instantly regretted not moving the body. Giving nothing away, Keith feigned disinterest. Julie was into drugs and other such things, he told the officers. They didn't seem convinced.

Arriving at the station, Keith was introduced to cops from Clark County, Washington. This was where the murder had taken place. As a suspect in the death of Julie, they asked Keith for a full confession. He lied. For the next five hours, he was grilled by the police. The longer the quizzing went on, the less evidence Keith was convinced they had. He was photographed, finger printed, and the police took hair and blood samples. DNA, Keith thought, was all over his crime scenes. But without enough evidence, the police turned him free. As the police took away the tarps from the truck and his log book, he figured he might have a few days left of freedom. Keith Jesperson needed to make plans.

Over the coming days, the scale of the problem began to dawn on Keith. There were a lot of witnesses who could attest to him being with Julie at the time of the murder. He considered fleeing to Canada. Still a Canadian citizen, it would at least give him some respite, plus Canada did not have the death penalty. But he couldn't depend on his trucking company to send him up there, as they were in league with the cops. Taking a bus would give the police plenty of time to intercept him, and when he looked through the window, there was a police car stationed outside the diner where he was drinking coffee.

Keith went to the nearest shop. He bought as much pain medicine as he could lay his hands on and retired to the truck, where he knew he had more. Getting undressed and worried that the police car outside would rush in and save his life, Keith debated whether or not he should write a note. But there was no explanation that would make the situation better. He swallowed all the pills as quickly as possible and laid back in the cabin. After an initial feeling like his eyeballs were expanding, he passed out.

It was raining when he woke up, and it was still night. Keith wasn't dead. He crawled to the truck stop restroom, and when he went to climb back into the cabin, someone hit him in the face. Looking around, he realized that he'd tried to get in the wrong truck. Dragging Keith into the offices, the driver deposited him in front of the security guard. Keith could barely speak, yet alone remember his name. He eventually tried to

103

explain the situation, enough that the guard just took his keys and told him to sober up. Suicide was never mentioned.

Back in the truck, Keith took the rest of the pills. He passed out, this time until midday. Waking up again, he realized that this was just another entry in the long list of things Keith Jesperson could never do right. Phoning up his employers, he found that he was now free to get back to work and argued with them about how they had turned the police on him. He hit the road, his mind racing for fresh ideas of how to kill himself. He tried again with sleeping pills but failed and considered wandering up a mountain and allowing himself to die of hypothermia. Instead, he wrote a letter to his brother confessing what he'd done. After that, Keith rang up the detective who'd arrested him and gave a full confession to the murder of Julie Winningham.

Keith Jesperson went to jail to await his trial. He was placed on suicide watch and didn't much like the people he was sharing his cell with. The other inmates didn't like him much either, due to the rape charges they overheard from an officer. Shunned, taunted, and threatened, he was moved to a solitary cell. A few days later, when talking with the cops again, all he could think about was the confession letter he'd sent to his brother and the Happy Face confessions he'd sent to the court houses and the newspapers. They might match up. He'd only confessed to Julie's murder. If they made the connection, he was doomed. While being flown across state lines, he resolved to call his brother at the first opportunity.

He was finally able to call Brad and immediately asked his brother to destroy the letter. But he was told that Les Jesperson, their dad, had already made Brad turn the letter over to the police. Keith was stunned. Les hadn't wanted to be accused of withholding evidence. Keith was visited by his kids. They were rushed away before they could really talk about much. As he was led back to his cells, Keith cried.

But as soon as Keith hit the stage in the court, he was a changed man. He seemed determined to right the wrongs of the court, who had convicted a couple of the murder of Taunja Bennett. He was furious that no one had responded to the confessions he had scrawled on the walls of restrooms. He accused the court of incompetence for their ability to address the Happy Face letters he had sent. It was like a one-an campaign to distract from the actual murders he had committed.

From his cell, Keith seemed happy to confess to more and more murders. At one point, he told his father that the actual figure stretched into three figures. Across the country, convicted killers began to chime up and insist that they had been convicted of Keith's crimes. But the courts refused to entertain such ideas. The only two that stuck around were the pair accused of murdering Taunja, and it took a series of smuggled press releases for the detectives to even consider the idea that the pair might have been falsely convicted. The cops seemed unwilling to overturn the case and even half-heartedly toured Keith around the murder site to try and see if he knew what he was talking about. It took Keith's discussions with journalist Phil Stanford to solve the case. Phil went and found the girl's missing purse following Keith's instructions. It would take another year before the court's overturned their initial decision.

Writing from jail, Keith began to sign letters with a Happy Face. Despite his lawyer's recommendations, he continued to talk to people on the outside and confessed to the crimes. He insisted on his own sanity and even drew diagrams to find the remains of the victims he said he had killed. He even managed to start a website from jail, where he sold a Self-Start Serial Killer Kit, which came with a free inflatable murdered woman.

Eventually, despite the fame Keith was trying to earn himself, the courts ruled against him. He was found guilty of eight counts of murder and sentenced to three consecutive life sentences. Originally serving his time in Oregon, he was transferred in 2009 while police investigated another potential victim of the Happy Face killer. To this day, he is still behind bars and is not likely to ever be released. After spending his life torturing animals, setting fires, and murdering women, Keith Hunter Jesperson is one long haul trucker who is never likely to hit the road ever again.

Conclusion

There are serial killer with higher body counts, and serial killers with more warped and twisted approaches to their crimes. But in Keith Hunter Jesperson, we have a somewhat unique opportunity to trace the lineage, development, methodology, and reasoning of a serial killer. The man himself, nowadays an unabashed self-publicist, is a fascinating figure. The figure who has become known as the Happy Face killer is entirely Keith's own creation. A savvy worker of the media, he knew how to steer the press into making him into something he was not. From the nervous, bullied young boy up to the feared serial killer, there is little in his supposed self-image that deals with the paranoia, the depression, and the resentment that drove Keith to commit murder.

Keith filled a strange niche in 1990s America. Before the rise of tracking technologies, a long haul trucker was essentially off the radar, provided with an excuse to be anywhere and nowhere at the same time. It was almost the perfect career for a serial killer, and it allowed him to remain on the loose for an incredibly long time. But, like many killers, he was eventually caught when his emotions trumped his reasoning. In his final act of murder, Keith Jesperson pushed his crimes too far. Now in jail, having escaped the death sentence, he is keen to chat about his crimes and happy to revel in the identity he has created for himself, the Happy Face killer. If you would like to read more about Keith's case or similar instances of serial killers in America, there is a further reading list that follows.

Further Reading

Berry-Dee, C. (2009). Dead men talking. London: John Blake.

Marriott, T. (2012). The evil within. London: Blake.

Mellor, L. (2012). Cold North killers. Toronto: Dundurn Press.

Moore, M. and Cook, M. (2009). Shattered silence. Springville, Utah: CFI.

Olsen, J. and Jesperson, K. (2002). I. New York: St. Martin's Press.

More Books from Jack Smith

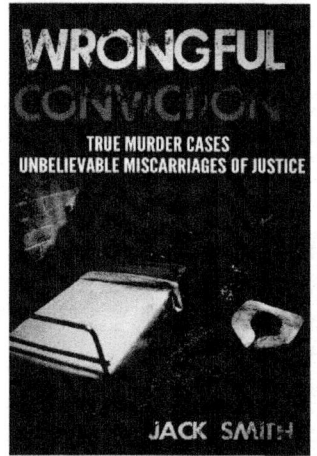

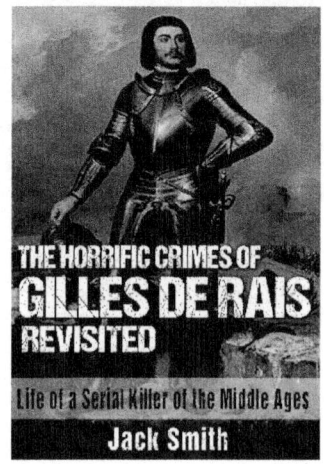

Printed in Great Britain
by Amazon

41136169R00066